EVEN
HAPPIER

EVEN HAPPIER

A Gratitude Journal for Daily Joy and Lasting Fulfillment

TAL BEN-SHAHAR, Ph.D.

New York   Chicago   San Francisco   Lisbon   London   Madrid   Mexico City
Milan   New Delhi   San Juan   Seoul   Singapore   Sydney   Toronto

The *McGraw·Hill* Companies

Library of Congress Cataloging-in-Publication Data

Ben-Shahar, Tal.
    Even happier : a gratitude journal for daily joy and lasting fulfillment /
Tal Ben-Shahar.
       p.   cm.
    ISBN 978-0-07-163803-6 (alk. paper)
    1. Gratitude.   2. Joy.   3. Happiness.   I. Title.

BF575.G68B46   2010
158—dc22   2009019024

5 6 7 8 9 10 11 12 13 14 15 16 17 18 19 20 21 22 QFR/QFR 1 5

ISBN 978-0-07-163803-6
MHID   0-07-163803-2

McGraw-Hill books are available at special quantity discounts to use as premiums and
sales promotions or for use in corporate training programs. To contact a representative,
please e-mail us at bulksales@mcgraw-hill.com.

To David, Shirelle, and Eliav—
for making each day even happier

ontents

Introduction

have often been asked by my students as well as by others who have read my books to collate the exercises that I present in my classes and writings. So here they are, in *Even Happier*.

When I was a psychology student, the classes that had the most impact on my life were ones that encouraged—or required—us to apply the material we studied to our personal lives. Not only did I benefit from these classes, but by putting ideas into practice I also internalized and memorized the material a lot better than I ever did in classes that just taught theory. Engaging in reflection and action—what I have called "ReflAction"—brings theory to life. I have adopted the practice of reflaction in my academic classes and public workshops, and I recommend that all teachers and students in any field who are concerned with real learning do the same.

This journal, which is a workbook or a playbook, can be used by individuals on their own as a guide and companion to help them apply to their daily lives the ideas of positive psychology that I discuss in *Happier* and *The Pursuit of Perfect*. The exercises can also be done jointly by a couple, with each holding the other accountable to the weekly or daily exercises, and then sharing ideas and feelings with one another. A group of people, as part of a book club, seminar, or workplace, can also embark together on the journey outlined in this book, and then get together once a week or once a month to discuss their insights and progress.

There is room in the pages of this book for you to write in. However, I recommend that you keep a separate notebook or a dedicated file on your computer for further reflection. The space in this journal should not in any way constrain your thoughts and feelings. You can gain much value from following the process outlined in this book (directly responding to the questions I pose) as well as from free association (writing about whatever comes to mind or heart).

Doing the exercises in this book can, in the words of Harvard professor David Perkins, foster *generative knowledge*, "knowledge that does not just sit there but functions richly in people's lives to help them understand and deal with the world." Personally engaging students or readers in the material contributes to their experience, growth, retention, and depth of understanding. This is precisely what I hope you will attain as you journey through this journal.

Enjoy!

EVEN
HAPPIER

On Being Grateful

Psychologists Robert Emmons and Michael McCullough conducted a series of studies in which they asked partici- pants to write down on a daily basis at least five things, major or minor, for which they were grateful. Participants' responses included everything from their parents to the Rolling Stones, from waking up in the morning to God. It turns out that putting aside a minute or two every day to express gratitude for one's life has far-reaching consequences. Compared with the control group, the grateful group not only became more appreciative of life in general but also enjoyed higher levels of well-being and positive emotions: they felt happier, more determined, more energetic, and more optimistic. They were also more generous and more likely to offer support to others. Finally, those who expressed gratitude also slept better, exercised more, and experienced fewer symptoms of physical illness.

I have been doing this exercise daily since September 19, 1999 (three years before Emmons and McCullough published their findings), when I heard Oprah tell her viewers to do it—and so I did! From around the time my son David turned three, we have been doing a variation of this exercise together. Every night I ask him, "What was fun for you today?" and then he asks me the same question. My wife and I regularly remind ourselves what we are grateful for in each other and in our relationship.

When we make a habit of gratitude, we no longer require a special event to make us happy. We become more aware of good things that happen to us during the day, as we anticipate putting them on our list. The gratitude list can include the name of a person you care about, something that you appreciate that you or someone else did, or an insight that you had as a result of writing in this journal.

What are the things that you are grateful for? What do you appreciate in your life?

....

....

....

....

....

....

....

....

EXERCISE

●●Daily Gratitude

Each day this week, write down at least five things for which you are grateful. The key when doing this exercise is to remain mindful, not to take this exercise for granted. One way of remaining mindful is by visualizing or reexperiencing whatever it is that you are writing down. For example, as you write down "parents," see them in your imagination; if you write down "conversation with partner," try to reexperience the same feelings you had while conversing with your partner.

After this week, during which I recommend you write down daily gratitudes, continue doing this exercise at least once a week. Because the benefits of doing this exercise are so significant, I have dedicated space in this journal for writing down your weekly gratitudes.

DAILY GRATITUDE LIST

DAY **1** I am grateful for:

DAY **2** I am grateful for:

DAY **3** I am grateful for:

DAY **4** I am grateful for:

DAY **5** I am grateful for:

DAY **6** I am grateful for:

DAY **7** I am grateful for:

"What you focus on expands, and when you focus on the goodness in your life, you create more of it. Opportunities, relationships, even money flowed my way when I learned to be grateful no matter what happened in my life."
    —Oprah Winfrey

Rituals

There is much research suggesting that change—learning new tricks, introducing a new behavior, replacing old habits—is extremely hard. Most attempts at change, whether by individuals or organizations, fail. In their book *The Power of Full Engagement*, Jim Loehr and Tony Schwartz provide a different way of thinking about change: they suggest that instead of focusing on cultivating *self-discipline* as a means toward change, we need to introduce *rituals*.

Initiating a ritual is often difficult, but maintaining it is relatively easy. Top athletes have rituals: they know that at specific hours during each day they are on the field, then in the gym, and then they stretch. For most of us, brushing our teeth at least twice a day is a ritual and therefore does not require special powers of discipline. We need to take the same approach toward any change we want to introduce.

According to Loehr and Schwartz, "Building rituals requires defining very precise behaviors and performing them at very specific times—motivated by deeply held values." For athletes, being a top performer is a deeply held value, and therefore they create rituals around training; for most people, cleanliness is a deeply held value, and therefore they create the ritual of brushing their teeth.

If we hold our personal happiness as a value and want to become happier, then we need to form rituals around that too.

What have you tried to change and did not succeed? What new behaviors or resolutions did you try to adopt and did not?

....
....
....
....
....
....
....

▓▓▓▓▓▓▓▓▓▓▓▓▓▓▓▓ **WEEKLY GRATITUDE LIST** ▓▓▓▓▓▓▓▓▓▓▓▓▓▓▓▓

This week, I am grateful for:...
....
....
....
....

▓▓

EXERCISE

Creating Rituals

Come up with two rituals that you believe would make you happier. It could be starting to meditate for fifteen minutes every evening, going on a date with your spouse on Tuesdays, taking four deep breaths first thing when you wake up in the morning, pleasure reading for an hour every other day, spending two hours each Sunday afternoon on your hobby, and so on.

Once you identify the rituals you want to adopt, enter them in your planner and begin to do them. New rituals may be difficult to initiate; over time, usually within as little as thirty days, performing these rituals will become as easy and as natural as brushing your teeth.

Throughout this journal, you will be encouraged to set rituals. Introduce no more than one or two rituals at a time and make sure they become a habit before you introduce new ones. As Tony Schwartz says, "Incremental change is better than ambitious failure.... Success feeds on itself."

....

....

....

....

....

....

....

....

"We are what we repeatedly do. Excellence, then, is not an act but a habit."

—Aristotle

Physical Activity

More and more studies in the area of mind-body medicine show the mental health benefits of physical exercise. Michael Babyak and his colleagues at Duke University Medical School, for example, showed that exercising three times a week for thirty minutes each time was as helpful for patients diagnosed with major depressive disorder as taking an antidepressant. Moreover, those who were on the drug were four times more likely to relapse into depression once the intervention ended than those who exercised.

Is exercising, then, like taking an antidepressant? Not exactly. In essence, *not exercising is like taking a depressant.* We have the need for exercise, and when this need is not fulfilled, we pay a price. We were not made to be inactive, sitting in front of a computer screen all day, or spending our days in meetings. We were made to run after an antelope for lunch, or run away from a lion so that we don't become lunch. We frustrate a physical need when we don't exercise, and when we frustrate a need—whether of vitamins, proteins, or exercise—we pay a price. John Ratey, a Harvard Medical School professor of psychiatry, says:

> In a way, exercise can be thought of as a psychiatrist's dream treatment. It works on anxiety, on panic disorder, and on stress in general, which has a lot to do with depression. And it generates the release of neurotransmitters—norepinephrine, serotonin, and dopamine—that are very similar to our most important psychiatric medicines. Having a bout of exercise is like taking a little bit of Prozac and a little bit of Ritalin, right where it is supposed to go.

And, I should add, with the potential positive side effects of increased self-esteem, improved mental functioning, a longer life span, better sleep, better sex, and a stronger immune system. Whether we suffer from depression or simply want to be happier, we should use this natural "wonder drug" more often.

Exercise, it must be stressed, is not a panacea, and sometimes drugs are important—each case of depression or anxiety is different, and some people may be helped by drugs and not by exercise.

How do you feel after exercising? What form of exercise do you enjoy most?

....

....

....

....

....

....

....

....

WEEKLY GRATITUDE LIST

This week, I am grateful for: ....

....

....

....

EXERCISE

●● Move It!

Commit to a ritual of physical exercise, beginning today. This month, you could start by going for a ten-minute walk three times a week. Next month, you could increase the time you spend exercising, until eventually, you are exercising four times a week for forty-five minutes each session. Below, write down your commitments for the next six months. You may want to contact a friend or a family member to embark on this ritual together, something that will significantly enhance your likelihood of staying the course.

_____

_____

_____

_____

_____

_____

_____

_____

_____

_____

_____

"It is exercise alone that supports the spirits, and keeps the mind in vigor."
—Cicero

The Work Paradox

In their article "Optimal Experience in Work and Leisure," Mihaly Csikszentmihalyi and Judith LeFevre show that people prefer leisure to work, a conclusion that no one would find startling. However, they also discovered something else: that people have more "flow" experiences at work. Flow is about being in "the zone," fully immersed in whatever it is that we are doing, performing at our best (peak performance), and enjoying ourselves (peak experience).

This paradox—that we say we prefer leisure at the same time that we are having our peak experiences at work—is strange and revealing. It suggests that our prejudices against work, our association of effort with pain and leisure with pleasure, is so deep-rooted that it distorts our perception of the actual experience. When we automatically and regularly evaluate positive experiences at work negatively, simply as a learned response, we are severely limiting our potential for happiness—because in order to be happy we must not only experience positive emotions but also evaluate them as such.

Can you learn to see your experience of school or work as a privilege? What do you enjoy in the experience? Are you able to enjoy it? Do you know people who exemplify a life of pleasurable work?

....

....

....

....

....

....

....

....

WEEKLY GRATITUDE LIST

This week, I am grateful for: ....

....

....

....

....

EXERCISE

Education Program

The happiest and most successful people are lifelong learners; they constantly ask questions and never cease to find wonder in the world around them. Regardless of where you are in your life journey—whether you are fifteen or one hundred and fifteen, whether you are a student or have worked in the same office for twenty-five years—create an education program for yourself.

Your program should include these two categories: personal development and professional development. Under each category, commit to learning material that will yield both present benefit and future benefit. Put aside regular times each day for your education.

For example, under the personal development category, you could commit to reading a chapter of Nathaniel Branden's *The Six Pillars of Self-Esteem* each day. For professional development, seek out a mentor you trust and ask him or her to join you for lunch, or attend a seminar on the latest developments in your industry.

Think about the relationship between these activities, the personal and the professional. Were there things about both that were enjoyable, and is there overlap between the two? If so, can you identify a common theme in both "work" and "pleasure" that you enjoy?

....

....

....

....

"In a culture that sometimes equates work with suffering, it is revolutionary to suggest that the best inward sign of vocation is deep gladness—revolutionary but true."

—Parker Palmer, *The Courage to Teach*

Meaning

Marva Collins was a schoolteacher in Chicago's inner city in the early 1970s, a place where crime and drugs were rampant and hope and optimism were scarce. In 1975 Collins founded a prep school for children in her neighborhood. The students, many of whom had been rejected from other schools and deemed unteachable, learned to read Shakespeare and Emerson by the fourth grade. For more than twenty years, Collins struggled financially to keep the school alive and was often on the verge of closing. But she never lost sight of her vision, recognizing happiness as the ultimate end. Reflecting on one of her students, Collins says, "It is worth all the sleepless nights wondering how I am going to balance our deficits to see the glow in [his] eyes that will one day light the world."

Collins could have made a fortune, and in the 1980s she was even offered a position as secretary of education, but she loved to teach and believed that she could make the most significant difference in the classroom. Teaching gave her life meaning that she believed no other profession could give her; teaching gave her the emotional gratification that no amount of money could buy. She felt she was "the wealthiest woman in the world" and that her experiences as a teacher were worth more to her than "all of the gold in Fort Knox" because happiness, not wealth or prestige, is the ultimate currency.

What, for you, is worth all of the gold in Fort Knox? If you can't think of anything you've already done that has that much meaning, can you envision something in your life that would provide that kind of wealth in the currency of happiness?

....

....

....

....

....

....

....

....

WEEKLY GRATITUDE LIST

This week, I am grateful for:...

....

....

....

EXERCISE

Create a Meaning Map

For a period of a week or two, keep a record of your daily activities. At the end of each day, write down how you spent your time, from a fifteen-minute session responding to e-mails to a longer, two-hour period of watching TV. This does not need to be a precise, minute-by-minute account of your day, but it should provide you with a sense of what your overall day looks like.

At the end of the week, create a table that has the name of the activity, how much meaning and pleasure it provides, and the amount of time you spent on it. Next to the amount of time, indicate whether you would like to spend more or less of your time on the activity. If you'd like to spend more time, write "+" next to it; if you'd like to spend a lot more time doing it, put down "++." If you'd like to spend less time on the activity, put a "−" next to it; for a lot less time, write "−−." If you are satisfied with the amount of time you are spending on a particular activity, or changing the amount of time you spend on it is not possible for one reason or another, write "=" next to it.

Are there things that you do not currently do that would yield high profits in the ultimate currency? Would going to the movies once a week contribute to your well-being? Would it make you happier to devote four hours a week to your favorite charity and to work out three times a week?

If you have many constraints and cannot introduce significant changes, make the most of what you have. What happiness boosters—brief activities that provide you both present and future benefits—could you introduce in your life? If a one-hour commute to work is uninspiring but unavoidable, try to infuse some meaning and pleasure in it. For example, listen to audio books or to your favorite music for part of the ride. Alternatively, take the train and use the time to read. As much as possible, ritualize these changes.

_____

_____

_____

_____

_____

_____

_____

_____

_____

_____

_____

_____

"The least of things with a meaning is worth more in life than the greatest of things without it." —Carl Jung

Benevolence

mmanuel Kant, the influential eighteenth-century German philosopher, tells us that for an act to have moral worth, it must be undertaken out of a sense of duty. When we act out of self-interest, then, we preclude the possibility of our action being a moral one.

Most philosophers and religions that advocate self-sacrifice as the foundation of morality, as Kant does, assume that acting in one's self-interest inevitably leads to acting against the interest of others—that if we do not fight our selfish inclinations, we will hurt others and disregard their needs.

What this worldview fails to acknowledge, however, is that we do not need to make a choice between helping others and helping ourselves. The two are not mutually exclusive. Helping oneself and helping others are inextricably intertwined: the more we help others, the happier we become; the happier we become, the more inclined we are to help others.

Think back to a time you helped someone. Try to reexperience the emotions you felt. Think about how giving and receiving are intertwined, two sides of the same coin. Are you open to giving to others? Are you open to receiving from others?

....

....

....

....

....

....

....

....

WEEKLY GRATITUDE LIST

This week, I am grateful for:...

....

....

....

....

EXERCISE

Meditating on Benevolence

Find a quiet spot. Sit down on a chair or the floor with your legs crossed. Make sure you are comfortable, with your back and neck straight. You can close your eyes or keep them open.

Enter a state of calm by breathing deeply through your nose or mouth, filling up the space of your belly with each breath, and slowly releasing the air through your nose or mouth.

Now, think back to a time when you behaved benevolently toward someone else and felt appreciated for it. In your mind's eye, see the person's response to your act. Savor it. Experience your own feelings; allow them to materialize inside you. As you see the other person and experience your own feelings, break the artificial divide that currently exists between helping yourself and helping others.

Now think about a future interaction with another person. It could be sharing an idea with a friend, giving flowers to a loved one, reading to your child, or donating to a cause you believe in. Experience the deep happiness that can come with each act of generosity. Regularly meditating on generosity contributes to our mental and physical health and actually makes us more generous.

In writing, commit to a number of benevolent acts, beyond what you are already doing.

_____

"*It is one of the most beautiful compensations of this life that no man can sincerely try to help another without helping himself.*"

—Ralph Waldo Emerson

Learning from Painful Experiences

We, especially in the United States, are often criticized for being a society obsessed with happiness: self-help books offering quick-fix solutions and a struggle-free life are selling at an unprecedented rate, with more and more people seeking psychiatric medication at the first sign of emotional discomfort. While the criticism is, to some extent, justified, it identifies the wrong obsession: the obsession is with pleasure, not with happiness.

The brave new world of quick fixes ignores our need for meaning. True happiness involves some emotional discomfort and difficult experiences, which some self-help books and psychiatric medication attempt to circumvent. Happiness presupposes our having to overcome obstacles. In the words of Viktor Frankl, "What man actually needs is not a tensionless state but rather the striving and struggling for some goal worthy of him. What he needs is not the discharge of tension at any cost, but the call of a potential meaning waiting to be fulfilled by him."

We should remember that going through difficult times can augment our capacity for pleasure: it keeps us from taking pleasure for granted, reminds us to be grateful for all the large and small pleasures in our lives. Being grateful in this way can *itself* be a source of real meaning and pleasure.

Think back to a difficult or painful experience you had. What did you learn from it? In what ways did you grow?

WEEKLY GRATITUDE LIST

This week, I am grateful for:

EXERCISE

Journaling About Hardship

Jamie Pennebaker from the University of Texas has demonstrated the benefits of coping with difficulties through writing. Every day for four consecutive days Pennebaker invited participants to spend fifteen to twenty minutes writing about upsetting or traumatic experiences. Participants were guaranteed confidentiality and were asked to open up as much as possible. It turns out that the one hour or so spent over a period of four days significantly reduced participants' overall levels of anxiety, increased their overall happiness, and improved their physical health.

On a separate sheet of paper, so that you are not constrained by space, spend fifteen to twenty minutes a day for four days following Pennebaker's instructions:

Write continuously about the most upsetting or traumatic experience of your entire life. Don't worry about grammar, spelling, or sentence structure. In your writing, I want you to discuss your deepest thoughts and feelings about the experience. You can write about anything you want. But whatever you choose, it should be something that has affected you very deeply. Ideally, it should be about something you have not talked about with others in detail. It is critical, however, that you let yourself go and touch those deepest emotions and thoughts that you have. In other words, write about what happened and how you felt about it, and how you feel about it now. Finally, you can write on different traumas during each session or the same one over the entire study. Your choice of trauma for each session is entirely up to you.

_____

"We are healed of a suffering only by expressing it to the full."

—Marcel Proust

Making Time

Time pressure is pervasive and, to some extent, accounts for the increase in rates of depression. One of my roles as a tutor during my six years of graduate school was to help college students with their résumés. It astounded me that each year, college students' accomplishments were more impressive than those of their predecessors, at least on paper. Initially, their awesome achievements impressed me—until I realized the emotional price they were paying for the smaller fonts and larger titles that were squeezed into the single page. In fact, in a survey of nationwide college students, 95 percent reported feeling "overwhelmed by everything they had to do."

We are too busy, trying to squeeze more and more activities into every day. Consequently, we fail to savor, to enjoy, potential sources of the ultimate currency that may be all around us—whether it is our work, a class, a piece of music, the landscape, our soul mate, or even our children.

What can we do, then, to enjoy our lives more despite the fast-paced rat-race environment so many of us live in? The answer contains both good news and bad. The bad news is that, unfortunately, there are no magic bullets. We must simplify our lives; we must slow down. The good news is that simplifying our lives, doing less rather than more, does not have to come at the expense of success.

In what areas or activities, if any, do you feel you are compromising on your happiness because of time pressure?

....

....

....

....

....

....

....

....

WEEKLY GRATITUDE LIST

This week, I am grateful for: ....

....

....

....

....

EXERCISE

Time Management

Write down the activities you were engaged in over the past week or two. Looking at the list, answer the following questions: Where can I simplify? What can I give up? Am I spending too much time on the Internet or watching TV? Can I reduce the number of meetings at work or the length of some of the meetings? Am I saying yes to activities to which I can say no?

Commit to reducing the busy-ness in your life. In addition, find time to dedicate yourself on a regular basis, fully and with undivided attention, to things you find both meaningful and pleasurable: spending time with your family, gardening, focusing on a project at work, meditating, watching a film, and so on.

....

....

....

....

....

....

....

....

....

....

....

....

"Simplicity, simplicity, simplicity! I say let your affairs be as two or three, and not a hundred or a thousand; instead of a million, count half a dozen."
—Henry David Thoreau

Enjoying the Journey

To expect *constant* happiness is to set yourself up for failure and disappointment. Not everything that we do can provide us both present and future benefit. It is sometimes worthwhile to forgo present benefit for greater future gain, and in every life some mundane work is unavoidable. Studying for exams, saving for the future, or being an intern and working eighty-hour weeks is often unpleasant, but it can help us to attain long-term happiness. The key, even as you forgo some present gain for the sake of a greater future gain, is to keep in mind that the objective is to spend as much time as possible engaged in activities that provide both present *and* future benefit.

Living as a hedonist, every now and then, has its benefits as well. As long as there are no long-term negative consequences (such as from the use of drugs), focusing solely on the present can rejuvenate us. In moderation, the relaxation, the mindlessness, and the fun that come from lying on the beach, eating pizza followed by a hot-fudge sundae, or watching television, can make us happier.

Think back to a time—a single experience or a longer period— when you enjoyed both present and future benefit.

....

....

....

....

....

....

....

....

WEEKLY GRATITUDE LIST

This week, I am grateful for: ....

....

....

....

EXERCISE

●● The Four Quadrants

On four consecutive days, spend at least fifteen minutes writing about a single experience or a period of time during which you resided in one of the four quadrants described in the following paragraphs. If you are moved to write more about a particular quadrant, do so, but do not write about more than one quadrant a day. Do not worry about grammar or spelling—just write! It is important that in your writing you include the *emotions* you experienced then or are experiencing at the moment, the particular *behaviors* you engaged in (i.e., describe what you did then), and the *thoughts* you had during the time or currently have as you write. Here are the particular instructions for each of the quadrants.

RAT RACER: Write about a period in your life when you felt as if you were constantly chasing some future goal, living in the rat race, unable to enjoy the day-to-day. Why were you doing what you were doing? What, if any, were some of the benefits to living that way? What, if any, was the price that you paid?

HEDONIST: Describe a period in your life when you lived as a hedonist or engaged in hedonic experiences, in which you sought immediate pleasure while ignoring the consequences of your actions. What, if any, were some of the benefits of living that way? What, if any, price did you pay?

NIHILIST: Write about a particularly difficult experience during which you felt nihilistic, resigned, or a longer period of time during which you felt helpless. Describe your deepest feelings and your deepest thoughts, ones you had or experienced then as well as ones that come up as you are writing.

HAPPY: Describe an extremely happy period in your life or a particularly happy experience. In your imagination, transport yourself to that time, try to reexperience the emotions, and then write about them.

....

....

....

....

....

....

....

....

....

....

....

....

"We are designed for the climb, not for taking our ease, either in the valley or at the summit." —John Gardner

Relationships: Knowing and Being Known

The high rate of divorce around the world sometimes occurs from a basic misunderstanding of what love is and what it entails. Most people mistake pure sexual desire (lust) for true love, and while sexual attraction is necessary for romantic love, it is not sufficient. No matter how "objectively" attractive one's partner is, or how much "subjective" attraction exists between the partners, the initial excitement, the purely physical attraction, wears off. Novelty excites our senses, and after a while, a live-in partner inevitably becomes familiar.

Familiarity, though, can have significant benefits too. While on the one hand it does lead to lower physical excitation, on the other hand familiarizing oneself with one's partner, getting to truly *know* him or her, can also lead to higher levels of intimacy— and through that to the growth of love as well as to better sex.

In his book *Passionate Marriage*, sex therapist David Schnarch challenges conventional wisdom in his field that reduces sex and passion to a form of physical, biological drive. If sex is indeed just that, then there is little hope for sustained, long-term passionate relationships. However, over decades of work with couples, Schnarch has demonstrated how sex can get better, if our focus is on getting to know our partner and to be known by him or her.

Schnarch points out how in order to cultivate genuine intimacy, the focus in a relationship has to shift from the desire to be validated to the desire to be known. Self-disclosure of our innermost self is crucial for sustaining love and passion in long-term relationships. We need to open up, share our deepest wants and fears, our sexual fantasies and life dreams. Being together, whether conversing in a restaurant or making love in the bedroom, becomes so much more meaningful and pleasurable when our focus shifts to knowing and being known.

Think of ways in which you can become known by your partner.
Think of ways in which you can get to know your partner.

WEEKLY GRATITUDE LIST

This week, I am grateful for:

EXERCISE

Positive Relationship

Relationship expert John Gottman is able to predict the success of a relationship based on how partners describe their shared past. If partners focus on the happy aspects of their time together, if they remember the past fondly, the relationship is much more likely to thrive. Focusing on meaningful and pleasurable experiences—in the past and the present—fortifies the connection and improves the relationship overall.

Write a positive history of your relationship, highlighting the meaningful and pleasurable experiences that you had together. You can write about how you met as well as about what you did yesterday. A positive focus can create a positive outcome. What can you do today, tomorrow, next week, and for the next ten or twenty years to bring more happiness to your relationship?

....
....
....
....
....
....

"All who could win joy must share it; happiness was born a twin."

—Byron

Learn to Fail or Fail to Learn

n their work on self-esteem, Richard Bednar and Scott Peterson point out that the very experience of coping—risking failure—increases our self-confidence. If we avoid hardships and challenges because we may fail, the message we are sending ourselves is that we are unable to deal with difficulty—in this case, unable to handle failure—and our self-esteem suffers as a result. But if we do challenge ourselves, the message we are sending ourselves, the message we internalize, is that we are resilient enough to handle potential failure. Taking on challenges instead of avoiding them has a greater long-term effect on our self-esteem than winning or losing, failing or succeeding.

Paradoxically, our overall self-confidence and our belief in our own ability to deal with setbacks may be reinforced when we fail, because we realize that the beast we had always feared—failure—is not as terrifying as we thought it was. Like the Wizard of Oz, who turns out to be much less frightening when he comes out from behind the curtain, failure turns out to be far less threatening when confronted directly. The pain associated with the fear of failure is usually more intense than the pain following an actual failure.

In her 2008 commencement speech at Harvard, J. K. Rowling, author of the Harry Potter books, talked about the value of failure:

> Failure meant a stripping away of the inessential. . . . I was set free, because my greatest fear had already been realized, and I was still alive, and I still had a daughter whom I adored, and I had an old typewriter and a big idea. And so rock bottom became the solid foundation on which I rebuilt my life. . . . Failure gave me an inner security that I had never attained by passing examinations. Failure taught me things about myself that I could have learned no other way. I discovered that I had a strong will, and more discipline than I had suspected; I also found out that I had friends whose value was truly above rubies. . . . The knowledge that you have emerged wiser and stronger from setbacks means that you are, ever after, secure in your ability to survive. You will never truly know yourself, or the strength of your relationships, until both have been tested by adversity.

We can only learn to deal with failure by actually experiencing failure, by living through it. The earlier we face difficulties and drawbacks, the better prepared we are to deal with the inevitable obstacles along our path.

Think of a challenge that you took on, something that you dared to do. What did you learn, and in what ways did you grow from the experience?

....

....

....

....

....

....

....

....

WEEKLY GRATITUDE LIST

This week, I am grateful for:..

....

....

....

EXERCISE

Keeping a Journal About Failure

In their work on mindfulness and self-acceptance, psychologists Shelley Carson and Ellen Langer note that "when people allow themselves to investigate their mistakes and see what mistakes have to teach them, they think mindfully about themselves and their world, and they increase their ability not only to accept themselves and their mistakes but to be grateful for their mistakes as directions for future growth." The following exercise is about investigating your mistakes.

Take fifteen minutes and write about an event or a situation in which you failed. Describe what you did, the thoughts that went through your mind, how you felt about it then, and how you feel about it now as you are writing. Has the passage of time changed your perspective on the event? What are the lessons that you have learned from the experience? Can you think of other benefits that came about as a result of the failure that made the experience a valuable one?

_____

_____

_____

_____

_____

_____

_____

_____

_____

_____

_____

"To dare is to lose one's footing momentarily. Not to dare, is to lose oneself."   —Søren Kierkegaard

Perfectionism and Optimalism

The key difference between the Perfectionist and the Optimalist is that the former essentially *rejects* reality while the latter *accepts* it.

The Perfectionist expects her path toward any goal—and, indeed, her entire journey through life—to be direct, smooth, and free of obstacles. When, inevitably, it isn't—when, for instance, she fails at a task, or when things don't quite turn out the way she expected—she is extremely frustrated and has difficulty coping. While the Perfectionist rejects failure, the Optimalist accepts it as a natural part of life and as an experience that is inextricably linked to success. She understands that failure to get the job she wanted or getting into a fight with her spouse is part and parcel of a full and fulfilling life; she learns what she can from these experiences and emerges stronger and more resilient. I was unhappy in college, in large part because I could not accept failure as a necessary part of learning—and living.

Perfectionists *reject reality* and replace it with a fantasy world—a world in which there is no failure and no painful emotions, a world in which their standards for success, no matter how unrealistic, can actually be met. Optimalists *accept reality*—they accept that in the real world some failure and sorrow is inevitable and that success has to be measured against standards that are actually attainable.

Perfectionists pay an extremely high emotional price for rejecting reality. Their rejection of failure leads to anxiety, because the possibility that they may fail is always there. Their rejection of painful emotions often leads to an intensification of the very emotion they are trying to suppress, ultimately leading to even more pain. Their rejection of real-world limits and constraints leads them to set unreasonable and unattainable standards for success, and because they can never meet these standards, they are constantly plagued by feelings of frustration and inadequacy.

Optimalists, on the other hand, derive great emotional benefit, and are able to lead rich and fulfilling lives, by accepting reality. Because they accept failure as natural—even if naturally they do not *enjoy* failing—they experience less performance anxiety and derive more enjoyment from their activities. Because they accept painful emotions as an inevitable part of being alive, they do not exacerbate them by trying to suppress them. They experience them, learn from them, and move on. Because they accept real-world limits and constraints, they set goals that they can actually attain and are thus able to experience, appreciate, and enjoy success.

Are there particular areas in your life where you tend to be an Optimalist? Are there areas in which you are more of a Perfectionist?

....

....

....

....

....

....

....

....

WEEKLY GRATITUDE LIST

This week, I am grateful for: ....

....

....

....

EXERCISE

●● Personality Traits Chart

Study the charts below, and for each characterization think of a few examples from your own life where you acted in accordance with one of these tendencies. Are there patterns you notice where you might change your approach? If you acted like a Perfectionist one time, can you think of how you might have done things differently if you had been thinking like an Optimalist?

Perfectionist	Optimalist
Rejects failure	*Accepts failure*
Rejects painful emotions	*Accepts painful emotions*
Rejects success	*Accepts success*
Rejects reality	Accepts reality

....

....

....

....

....

....

....

....

....

....

....

"In the depth of winter, I finally learned that there was within me an invincible summer."
　　　　　　　　　　　　　　　　　　　—Albert Camus

The 80/20 Rule

Italian economist Vilfredo Pareto was the first to introduce the 80/20 rule—pointing out that, in general, 20 percent of the population of a country owns 80 percent of the country's wealth, that 20 percent of a company's clients generates 80 percent of its revenues, and so on. More recently, the 80/20 rule, also known as the Pareto Principle, has been applied to time management by Richard Koch and Marc Mancini, who suggest that we can make better use of our time by investing our efforts in the 20 percent that will get us 80 percent of the results we want to achieve. For example, it may take between two and three hours to write that perfect report, but in thirty minutes we may be able to produce a report that is sufficiently good for our purpose.

In college, once I stopped being a Perfectionist who needed to read every word in every book that my professors assigned, I began to apply the Pareto Principle, skimming most of the assigned readings but then identifying and focusing on the 20 percent of the text that would yield the most "bang for the buck." I still wanted to do well academically. That much hadn't changed. What did change was my "A or nothing" approach that had guided me as a Perfectionist. While my grade-point average did initially suffer slightly, I was able to devote more time to important extracurricular activities such as playing squash, developing my career as a public speaker, and, last but not least, spending time with my friends. I ended up not only a great deal happier than I had been during my first two years in college but also, looking at that period in my life as a whole (as opposed to through the narrow lens of my grade point average), more successful. The 80/20 rule has continued to serve me well in my career.

Think about your 80/20 allocation of time. Where can you do less? Where do you want to invest more?

....

....

....

....

....

....

....

....

WEEKLY GRATITUDE LIST

This week, I am grateful for:...

....

....

....

EXERCISE

●●●Integrity Mirror

Make a list of the things that are most meaningful and pleasurable to you, that make you happiest. For example, the list could include family, exercising, promoting individual rights around the world, listening to music, and so on.

Next to each of the items on your list write down how much time per week or month you devote to it. Now ask yourself whether you are living your highest values. Are you spending quality time with your partner and children? Are you exercising three times a week? Are you active in an organization committed to the spread of freedom? Do you put time aside to listen to music at home and to attend concerts?

Now think about the 80/20 principle and how it can be applied to this list. Look at all your priorities and decide which 20 percent is going to give you 80 percent satisfaction.

This exercise raises a mirror to our lives and helps us determine whether or not there is congruence—integrity—between our highest values and the way we live. With increased integrity comes increased happiness.

_____

....

....

....

....

....

....

....

....

....

....

....

....

....

....

....

"The best way you can predict your future is to create it."

—Stephen Covey

Self-Perception

R esearch by psychologist Daryl Bem shows that we form attitudes about ourselves in the same way that we form attitudes about others, namely, through observation. If we see
a man helping others, we conclude that he is kind; if we see a
woman standing up for her beliefs, we conclude that she is prin-
cipled and courageous. Similarly, we draw conclusions about
ourselves by observing our own behavior. When we act kindly
or courageously, our attitudes are likely to shift in the direction
of our actions, and we tend to feel, and see ourselves as, kinder
and more courageous. Through this mechanism, which Bem calls
Self-Perception Theory, behavior can change attitudes over time.
And since *perfectionism is an attitude*, we can begin to change it
through our behavior.

Think about recurring behaviors in your life, be they toward others or relating to you alone. What conclusion about yourself do you derive from observing these behavioral patterns?

....

....

....

....

....

....

....

....

WEEKLY GRATITUDE LIST

This week, I am grateful for:...

....

....

....

EXERCISE

Taking Action

Think of something that you would like to do but have always been reluctant to try for fear of failing. Then go ahead and do it! Audition for a part in a play, try out for a sports team, ask someone out on a date, start writing that article or book that you've always wanted to write. As you pursue the activity, and elsewhere in your life, behave in ways that an Optimalist would, even if initially you have to fake it. Look for additional opportunities to venture outside your comfort zone, ask for feedback and help, admit your mistakes, and so on. Notice your feelings, thoughts, and behaviors as you exit your comfort zone.

_____

_____

_____

_____

_____

_____

_____

_____

_____

_____

_____

"The way to get started is to quit talking and begin doing."
—Walt Disney

Permission to Be Human

We often learn early on to hide and suppress our feelings, the pleasurable as well as the painful ones. We may have been told that boys don't cry, that experiencing or expressing pleasure and joy at our accomplishments was evidence of sinful pride, or that wanting something that someone else had was greedy and unbecoming. We may have been taught that being attracted to someone and yearning to express that physically was dirty and shameful, or, conversely, that feeling shy and nervous about opening ourselves up emotionally and physically was uncool and shameful. Unlearning the lessons of childhood and early adulthood is hard, which is why it is difficult for so many of us to open ourselves to the flow of emotions.

While we do not have to openly and publicly display our feelings, we should, when possible, provide a channel for the expression of our emotions. We can talk to a friend about our anger and anxiety, write in our journal about our fear or jealousy, join a support group of people who are struggling with issues similar to ours, and, at times, in solitude or in the presence of someone who cares about us, allow ourselves to shed a tear—of sorrow or of joy.

Can you think of early experiences that taught you to express emotions or suppress them? What are some of the outlets in your life for the expression of emotions, painful and pleasurable ones?

....

....

....

....

....

....

....

....

....

▓▓▓▓▓▓▓▓▓▓▓ WEEKLY GRATITUDE LIST ▓▓▓▓▓▓▓▓▓▓▓

This week, I am grateful for:..

....

....

....

....

EXERCISE

Experiencing the Experience

You can use the power of mindfulness to unlock the hold of painful emotions. Tara Bennett-Goleman, a therapist who brings together Eastern and Western psychology, writes: "Mindfulness means seeing things as they are, without trying to change them. The point is to dissolve our reactions to disturbing emotions, being careful not to reject the emotion itself. By focusing on a painful emotion, accepting it with an open heart and mind, and letting it flow through us, we can help it dissolve, disappear."

For example, if you get extremely nervous in front of an audience, close your eyes and imagine yourself on stage; if you lost someone and time has not healed the pain, imagine yourself sitting next to the deceased or saying good-bye to him. You can also bring up certain emotions, from insecurity to sadness, by thinking about them without imagining a particular situation. Once the emotion comes up, just stay with the experience for a few minutes without trying to change it.

Throughout this exercise, to the extent possible, maintain deep, gentle breathing. If your mind wanders, return to whatever it is that you were imagining or experiencing, and continue with the breathing. If tears come up, let them flow; if other emotions such as anger or disappointment or joy come up, let them be. If a particular part of your body reacts in a certain way—a knot in the throat or an increased heartbeat—you can shift your attention to that part and imagine yourself breathing into it, without trying to change it.

This exercise is about giving yourself the permission to feel, to experience the experience rather than to ruminate on it; it is about accepting the emotions as they are, being with them rather than trying to understand and "fix" them.

"Those who don't know how to weep with their whole heart don't know how to laugh either."
—Golda Meir

Integrity

ntegrity is defined as "the quality or condition of being whole or undivided." People have integrity when no schism or division exists between what they say and what they do, when there is congruence between their words and their actions. Integrity is about a political leader following up on her preelection promises to her constituents, and it's about being on time for a lunch meeting with a friend. The words that the politician utters to millions of people are important, as are the words that we utter to our friend committing ourselves to be at a particular place at a particular time.

No one is perfect; every person has been late for an appointment, and every person has, at some time or another, failed to fulfill a commitment. The question, therefore, isn't whether or not a person has integrity, but the degree to which a person is integrated. Each person is somewhere on the continuum between being perfectly integrated and perfectly disintegrated. At one extreme of the continuum we have those who do their utmost to be true to their word, who are committed to their commitments;

at the other extreme, we find those who perceive the commitments they make as little more than noise coming out of their mouths. Where we are on the continuum determines, to a great extent, the respect that others have for us and, more important, the respect that we have for ourselves.

When I follow up on my commitments—to others or to myself—I am sending others and myself an important message: that my thoughts, my words, and my self matter. My words are an expression of my self, and therefore when I honor my words I am honoring my self.

The psychologist Nathaniel Branden, considered the father of the self-esteem movement, recognizes integrity as one of the essential pillars of self-esteem. Research by Branden and others suggests the existence of a self-reinforcing loop between integrity and self-esteem.

The more integrity we practice, the more we esteem ourselves; and the more self-esteem we have, the more likely we are to exemplify congruence between our words and our actions.

Can you think of particular people who exemplify high levels of integrity? Where in your life would you like to increase your integrity?

....

....

....

....

....

....

....

....

....

WEEKLY GRATITUDE LIST

This week, I am grateful for: ....

....

....

....

....

EXERCISE

Practicing Integrity

One of the most potent ways for building our self-esteem is to practice integrity. We can begin by committing to being on time for every meeting in the coming week; by writing down the promises we make—to call a friend back, to help our colleague at work, or to take our kids out for a movie—and then making sure that we deliver on our promises; or by exercising three times a week and eating healthfully for six days out of the week as we said we would.

At the end of the week we can look back, reflect, and draw our lessons. For example, where was I on the integrity continuum? Are there any particular domains—my family life or professional life, for instance—where I compromise my integrity more than in other domains? Which commitments have I made that I was unable to fulfill? Did I overcommit, and, if so, when do I need to learn to say no? After we have integrated the lessons we've learned from the week, we can commit to another week of practicing integrity.

When we commit to this exercise of integrity, we must do so gradually. Just as we would not embark on a physical training regimen by running ten miles a day, so too should we not expect to be able to lead a fully integrated life overnight. Integrity takes time to cultivate, and we must be prepared for an ongoing, lifelong process of continuous improvement. While it will only take a week or two before we begin to notice an increase in our self-esteem and in the respect that others have for us, it will take months or even years of conscious *effort* for integrity to become second nature, a way of life.

....

....

....

....

....

....

....

....

....

....

....

....

....

"Happiness can be built only on virtue, and must of necessity have truth for its foundation."
—Samuel Taylor Coleridge

Peak Experiences

The term *peak experience*, according to psychologist Abraham Maslow, refers to "the best moments of the human being, for the happiest moments of life, for experiences of ecstasy, rapture, bliss, of the greatest joy." These moments can come from "profound aesthetic experiences such as creative ecstasies, moments of mature love, perfect sexual experiences, parental love, experiences of natural childbirth, and many others." These highs do not last for long; however, experiencing them can have lasting consequences. They can help us gain insight into who we are and what we are about, provide us with the courage and confidence to go through difficult periods in the future, inspire and motivate us to do things we would not have done otherwise, make us more resilient as well as happier.

Think back to a peak experience or two. What can you do to enjoy more peak experiences in your life?

....

....

....

....

....

....

....

....

▬▬▬▬▬▬▬▬▬ WEEKLY GRATITUDE LIST ▬▬▬▬▬▬▬

This week, I am grateful for:..

....

....

....

....

EXERCISE

Reliving Peak Experiences

Peak experiences can be the genesis of change and can actually transform our lives as a whole. One of the ways to extend their impact beyond the temporary high is to follow the protocol of a study run by psychologists Chad Burton and Laura King. Participants in the study were called in and asked to write about their peak experiences for fifteen minutes at a time over three days. Subsequently, participants enjoyed greater physical as well as mental health compared to a control group that did not go through the same exercise. These are the instructions that participants received:

> Think of the most wonderful experience or experiences in your life, happiest moments, ecstatic moments, moments of rapture, perhaps from being in love, or from listening to music, or suddenly "being hit" by a book or painting or from some great creative moment. Choose one such experience or moment. Try to imagine yourself at that moment, including all the feelings and emotions associated with the experience. Now write about the experience in as much detail as possible trying to include the feelings, thoughts, and emotions that were present at the time. Please try your best to reexperience the emotions involved.

Put aside fifteen minutes on three days this week and follow the above instructions. So that you don't feel constrained by space, write on a separate piece of paper. On the second and third day, you can either write about the same experience you wrote about on day one or a different experience.

....

....

....

....

....

....

....

....

....

....

....

....

"I have often thought that the best way to define a man's character would be to seek out the particular mental or moral attitude in which, when it came upon him, he felt himself most deeply and intensively active and alive. At such moments, there is a voice inside which speaks and says, 'This is the real me.'"

—William James

Relationships: Gridlock

According to sex therapist David Schnarch, every long-term relationship, sooner or later, experiences what he refers to as gridlock: the point at which couples feel stuck in a conflict and see no way out. This is not just a regular conflict that is easily resolved or forgotten but an intense and recurring conflict that seems unsolvable. These recurring conflicts usually revolve around issues relating to children, in-laws, money, or sex. What kind of education should the children receive? What is the desirable frequency of sexual relations, and what turns each partner on? Gridlock often challenges the sense of self of one or both partners, because it confronts them with a choice between integrity (holding on to their beliefs) and getting along with their partner by compromising.

It is not uncommon for relationships that reach such a point to come to an end—either in the form of divorce, or if for one reason or another the partners choose to remain legally bound, they are spiritually, physically, and emotionally apart. What Schnarch suggests, though, is that gridlock is a critical point, an opportunity for personal and interpersonal growth: "Marriage operates at much greater intensity and pressure than we expect—so great, in fact, couples mistakenly assume it's time for divorce when it's really time to get to work." Partners who successfully overcome gridlock emerge stronger as individuals and as a couple; their relationship becomes more authentic and intimate.

One of the most important ways of cultivating intimacy and depth within a relationship—of getting to know, and to be known by, our partner—is through dealing with interpersonal problems, which Schnarch refers to as "the drive wheels and grind stones of intimate relationships." Deviations from the straight line are not indicative of an inherent flaw in one of the partners or the relationship, but rather are part of the process, with the general direction being toward greater acceptance, intimacy, and passion.

Think of a time you felt stuck in a relationship. What did you do, or could you have done, to emerge stronger from the gridlock?

This week, I am grateful for: ....

....

....

....

....

EXERCISE

●● Sentence Completion

Psychologist Nathaniel Branden has developed an exercise called sentence completion, which is about generating a number of endings to an incomplete sentence. The key to doing this exercise is to generate *at least* six endings to each sentence stem, either aloud or in writing. When doing this exercise, it is important to set aside your critical faculties and to write or say whatever comes to mind, whether or not it makes sense and regardless of internal contradictions and inconsistencies. You can repeat the same sentence stems each day this week or come up with your own stems.

So that you are not constrained by space, on a separate sheet of paper write down one sentence stem at a time and generate as many endings as you can think of in a minute or two. After you have completed all the stems, you can go over your responses and identify the ones that make sense to you, the ideas you would like to explore further, and the ones that are irrelevant. In the space allotted for reflection below, you can analyze the endings, write about what you have learned from some of them, and commit to taking action based on your analysis.

Some of the stems relate to a particular person (for X, write the name of a person you care about), and others focus on relationships in general.

- *To improve my relationship with X by 5 percent . . .*
- *If I open myself up 5 percent more . . .*
- *To create more intimacy in my relationship . . .*
- *If I accept X 5 percent more . . .*
- *If I accept myself 5 percent more . . .*
- *To improve the relationship I have with myself . . .*
- *To bring more love to my life . . .*
- *I am beginning to see that . . .*

....
....
....
....
....
....
....
....
....
....
....

"Love is everything it's cracked up to be. . . . It really is worth fighting for, being brave for, risking everything for." —Erica Jong

Acts of Kindness

The person who contributes to others derives so much benefit from his action that I often think that there is no more selfish act than a generous act. While the rewards of generosity as a way of life may or may not come in the form of material success, they always pay dividends in the ultimate currency. Happiness is an unlimited resource—there is no fixed pie, and one person's gain does not entail another person's loss; it is through generosity—giving and sharing as a way of life—that we can best tap the infinite reserve of spiritual and emotional wealth.

The emotional and spiritual reward of generosity comes from the act of giving itself. Our nature is such that there are fewer more satisfying acts than sharing with others, than feeling that we have contributed to the lives of other people. For proof of our benevolent nature, all we need to do is think back to the last time we helped someone, to a time when we made a positive difference in someone else's life. The satisfaction most of us derive from the act of giving—in and of itself and independent of external rewards—is immense.

When is the last time you helped someone? Whether it was a large gesture or something small that brightened another person's day, how did it make you feel?

....

....

....

....

....

....

....

....

WEEKLY GRATITUDE LIST

This week, I am grateful for:..

....

....

....

EXERCISE

•●● Performing Acts of Kindness

Psychologist Sonja Lyubomirsky asked participants in a study to commit a few acts of kindness during each week, whether for strangers or people they knew, whether openly or secretly, whether spontaneously or planned. The participants enjoyed a significant increase in their well-being. The most benefit was derived by those who were asked to constantly vary their acts of kindness and who carried out their acts on one day during the week rather than spreading them thinly over the week.

On any one day during this week, perform at least five acts of kindness, beyond what you normally do. These do not have to be grand acts (though if you can do something to bring about world peace that would be great). For example, help your friend with the laundry, donate to a cause in which you believe, open a door for a stranger, write a thank-you note, give blood, and so on. Below, write down what you did and also what you plan to do next week.

....

....

....

....

....

....

....

....

....

....

....

....

"Thousands of candles can be lighted from a single candle, and the life of the candle will not be shortened. Happiness never decreases by being shared."
—Buddha

Benefit Finding

How is it that some people who have every conceivable reason to be happy, who have fulfilled their dreams and attained success, are miserable, whereas others, who repeatedly face misfortune and hardship, rarely fail to celebrate life? The reason behind this baffling (though common) phenomenon is that our happiness is not only a function of the objective *events* that make up our lives but also of the subjective way we *interpret* them.

An event can be anything from winning a championship to getting a C on an exam, from striking it rich to being rejected by our partner. How we experience these events is largely determined by our interpretation and what we decide to focus on: Do I celebrate my victories and accomplishments, or do I take them for granted and then lament the fact that I did not perform perfectly? Do I reproach myself for a poor grade and for being rejected, or do I focus on the lessons that I can learn from the experience?

No person is immune to feelings of sadness or pain. But there are those who seem to be able to find the good in a situation—they rejoice in their own as well as in others' accomplishments, have a knack for turning setbacks into opportunities, and go through life with an overall sense of optimism. Then there are others, who always see the glass as being half-empty, rarely find a reason to be happy, always seem dissatisfied, and generally go through life with a sense of morbid pessimism.

In the first example, we find the archetype of the *benefit finder*— that person who finds the silver lining in a dark cloud, who makes lemonade out of lemons, who looks on the bright side of life, and who does not fault a writer for using too many clichés. The second archetype is what Henry David Thoreau calls the *fault finder* who "will find faults even in paradise." The fault finder will be unhappy no matter what.

While I do not believe that things just happen for the best, I do believe that some people are able to make the best out of things that happen. The notion that things just happen for the best is passive; the notion that we make the best out of things that happen is active.

For fault finders, no success can ever bring lasting happiness, and failure is used to confirm their bleak outlook on life. In contrast, those who learn to focus on the positive can derive benefit from both failure and success; wherever benefit finders turn, they see opportunities for growth and celebration.

Do you consider yourself more of a benefit finder or a fault finder?
In which areas in your life are you more of a benefit finder?

....

....

....

This week, I am grateful for: ....

....

....

....

....

EXERCISE

Cognitive Reconstruction

Cognitive reconstruction can help us shift toward becoming benefit finders. Cognitive reconstruction reminds us to look beyond the negative consequences of a failure—to take the time to ask ourselves what we have learned from the experience, albeit a difficult one, and how we can grow from it.

Write about a few events in your life, first as a fault finder, then as a benefit finder. For example, writing about an exam you failed, first write about how upset you were and what a painful experience it was (fault finder), and then write about how that failure humbled you and taught you the importance of hard work (benefit finder). In writing about the events, remember that being a benefit finder is not about things necessarily happening for the best—or about being happy regardless of what happens to us—but rather about accepting what has happened as a fact and then making the best of it.

....

....

....

....

....

....

....

....

....

....

....

....

"A pessimist sees the difficulty in every opportunity; an optimist sees the opportunity in every difficulty." —Winston Churchill

Saying "Thank You"

Expressing gratitude to others—to our parents, teachers, friends, students—is among the most effective ways of raising others', as well as our own, levels of well-being. Professor Martin Seligman introduced the *gratitude visit* exercise as part of his Positive Psychology class, asking students to write a letter expressing their appreciation to a person who helped them in some way, and then visiting the person and reading the letter aloud. The effect of this exercise, as reported by Seligman and his students, and indeed as confirmed by subsequent research, is remarkable—in terms of the benefit it brings to the giver, the recipient, and their relationship.

I have assigned similar exercises in my classes and have on a number of occasions been moved to tears when students reported back. A father hugged his child for the first time in over a decade, a friendship that had seemingly died years earlier was resurrected, an old coach came away from the meeting looking younger than he had in years. The power of gratitude is immense, and while there are many ways to express gratitude, personally delivering a letter of gratitude, and then reading it aloud, is especially powerful.

Think of a person whom you appreciate. What do you appreciate in that person; what are you grateful for?

....

....

....

....

....

....

....

....

WEEKLY GRATITUDE LIST

This week, I am grateful for: ....

....

....

....

EXERCISE

Gratitude Visit

Write a letter to someone you appreciate, expressing your gratitude to that person. Refer to particular events and experiences, to things that he or she did for which you are grateful. Writing a gratitude letter is much more than writing thank-you notes, which are certainly important and ought to be distributed in abundance. A gratitude letter is a thoughtful examination of the meaning and pleasure that you derive from the relationship; it includes particular experiences that provided joy as well as shared dreams that are significant.

A single letter of gratitude boosts our levels of well-being, but for the writer this spike is usually temporary. For letters of gratitude and gratitude visits to have a more lasting effect, they would have to become a ritual. Ideally, we should write a weekly letter. However, a monthly letter is certainly a lot better than no letter at all. There is benefit just in writing the letter, but the value is increased if you actually send the letter or, better yet, deliver it in person.

Write down the names of at least five people you appreciate, and commit to actual dates when you will be writing and delivering gratitude letters to them.

....

....

....

....

....

....

....

....

....

....

....

....

"Gratitude is not only the greatest of virtues, but the parent of all others."
—Cicero

Recovery

We have a primal need for pleasure and recreation—but, as humans with free will, we can choose to ignore this need, to overcome our instincts and go against our nature. We convince ourselves that there is no limit to how far we can push ourselves, that just as science produces better, faster, more reliable and steady machines, we too can hone our abilities through modifying our nature. Many of us attempt to train ourselves to need less down time—to sleep less, to rest less, to cease less—to do more and stretch ourselves beyond our limits. But, like it or not, there is a limit, and if we continue to violate nature's demands, to abuse ourselves, we will pay the price—individually and as a society.

The rising levels of mental health problems, coupled with improved psychiatric medication, are thrusting us toward a brave new world. To reverse direction, rather than listening to advertisers who promise us wonder drugs, we need to listen to our nature and rediscover its wonders. Regular recovery can often do the work of psychiatric medicine, only naturally.

Are you getting enough recovery time? Do you take enough breaks during the day? Are you getting sufficient sleep each night? Do you take a day off once a week? When was your last vacation? When is the next one?

....

....

....

....

....

....

....

....

....

WEEKLY GRATITUDE LIST

This week, I am grateful for:..

....

....

....

....

EXERCISE

Learning from Your Best Past

Write about a period—anywhere between a month and a year—when you thrived at work, when, in comparison to other times, you felt yourself most satisfied, productive, creative. If you have not worked for long enough, or cannot think of such a period, write about another time when you thrived—at school, for instance.

What was it about what you did then that led you to thrive? What form of recovery did you have in place? Who did you work with? Most important, what can you learn from what you did then, and how can you apply it to what you are doing now or will be doing in the future?

In writing, commit to possible steps that you can take to bring out the best in you. In your diary, enter recovery sessions in the form of regular gym classes, outings with friends, and longer vacations with your family.

Just as you look at your own experiences, look at other people—at work or elsewhere. Ask yourself what you can learn from them, in terms of what you want to do and how you want to be, as well as in terms of what you would like to avoid.

"He enjoys true leisure who has time to improve his soul's estate."
—Henry David Thoreau

Relationships: Accentuating the Positive

The initial stages of a relationship—courtship, marriage, honeymoon—are usually relatively conflict-free. But then, for as long as the couple is together, there is conflict. To many, conflict within a relationship means that the relationship itself is in trouble; perfect harmony—the absence of conflict—is considered the standard we should all strive for.

As it turns out, conflict is not only unavoidable but actually *crucial* for the long-term success of the relationship. Think of conflicts as a form of vaccine. When we immunize against a disease, we are in fact injecting a weakened strain of the disease into the body, which is then stimulated to develop the antibodies that enable it to deal with more major assaults later on. Likewise, minor conflicts help our relationship develop defense capabilities;

they immunize the relationship and subsequently help partners deal with major gridlocks when they arise.

Psychologist John Gottman, who has for many years researched thriving and failing relationships, has shown that couples in successful long-term relationships enjoy a five-to-one ratio between positive and negative events. For every expression of anger or criticism or hostility there are five instances where the partners act kindly to each other, show empathy, make love, express interest, or display affection toward one another.

While Gottman found the ideal relationship at the five-to-one ratio point, we should keep in mind that the ratio is an average across many relationships. There are successful relationships where the ratio is three-to-one and others where it is ten-to-one. The key messages from Gottman's research are, first, that some negativity is vital, and second, that it is essential to have more positivity than negativity. Little or no conflict within a relationship indicates that the partners are not dealing with important issues and differences. Given that no person or partnership is perfect, absence of conflict indicates that the partners are avoiding challenges, running away from confrontations rather than learning from them. At the same time, while conflict is important, relationships that do not contain significantly more kindness and affection than harshness and anger are unhealthy.

Do you find yourself criticizing your partner as much as or more than you compliment or praise him or her? What benefits do you think would come from instilling the relationship with more positive messages and behaviors?

....

....

....

....

....
....
....
....
....

▓▓▓▓▓▓▓▓▓ WEEKLY GRATITUDE LIST ▓▓▓▓▓▓▓▓▓

This week, I am grateful for:...

....
....
....
....

EXERCISE

●●●Pleasure Points

Gottman's advice to couples, beyond striving to higher levels of respect and acceptance, is that they should accentuate the positive aspects of the relationship. Accentuating the positive does not necessarily require radical change and transformation. Peter Fraenkel of the Ackerman Institute for the Family recommends introducing "sixty-second pleasure points." Fraenkel suggests that rather than relying primarily on special events or special gifts to sustain a relationship, each partner should initiate as few as three pleasure points each day. A passionate kiss, a thoughtful, funny e-mail or an amorous text message, a simple "I love you"—all these can go a long way toward sustaining and cultivating love. Heartfelt compliments are important, too.

Come up with a list of sixty-second pleasure points and, in writing, commit to at least three of them per day for the next week. They can be different ones each day or the same, but the goal is to make sure you come up with enough to last for a week.

....

....

....

....

....

....

....

....

....

....

....

"I can live for two months on a good compliment." —Mark Twain

Cognitive Therapy

The basic premise of cognitive therapy is that we react to our interpretation of events rather than directly to the events themselves, which is why the same event may elicit radically different responses from different people. An event leads to a thought (an interpretation of an event), and the thought in turn evokes an emotion. I see a baby (event), recognize her as my daughter (thought), and feel love (emotion). I see the audience waiting for my lecture (event), interpret it as threatening (thought), and experience anxiety (emotion).

Event ➡ Thought ➡ Emotion

The goal of cognitive therapy is to restore a sense of realism by getting rid of distorted thinking. When we identify an irrational thought (a cognitive distortion), we change the way we think about an event and thereby change the way we feel. For example, if I experience paralyzing fear before a job interview, I can evaluate the thought that elicits the anxiety (if I am rejected, it will all be over and I will never find a job) and reinterpret the event by disputing and replacing the distorted evaluation with a rational one (although I really want this job, there are many other desirable jobs out there). The distortion elicits an intense and unhealthy fear of failure; the rational thought reframes the situation and potentially poses a healthy challenge.

Reflect on an intense emotional reaction that you have had to a particular situation. Was your reaction appropriate? Is there another way of interpreting the situation?

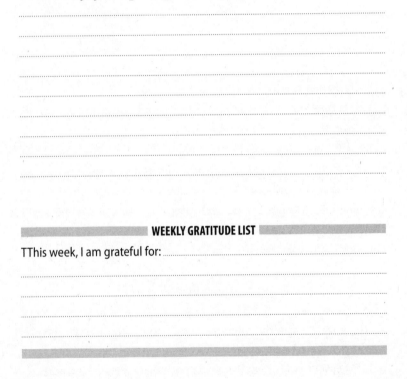

WEEKLY GRATITUDE LIST

TThis week, I am grateful for:

EXERCISE

●◗ The PRP Process

One of the most useful methods that I have found for dealing with disturbing emotions is to follow the PRP process: giving myself the *permission* to be human, cognitively *reconstructing* the situation, and gaining a wider *perspective*.

Think of a recent event that has upset you emotionally, or think of an upcoming event that you are worried about. Begin by giving yourself the *permission* to be human: acknowledge what happened as well as the emotion that you are feeling as a result. Feel free to talk to someone you trust or to write down how you feel, or, if you prefer, give yourself the time and space to experience the experience. This stage can last five seconds or five minutes or more, as appropriate.

Reconstruct the situation. Ask yourself what positive outcomes the event had. This does not mean that you are happy about what happened but simply that there are benefits that can be derived. Did you learn something new? Have you gained a new insight into yourself or others? Have you become more empathic? Are you more appreciative of what you have in life?

Finally, take a step back and gain a wider *perspective* on the situation. Can you see the experience in the larger scheme of things? How will you see the situation a year from now? Are you sweating the small stuff?

Progressing through the PRP process does not have to be linear: you can move from permission to perspective, then to reconstruction, then back to permission again, and so on.

Repeat this exercise on a regular basis, either by actively looking for an experience that happened or by responding to experiences as they happen. The more you practice, the more benefit you will derive from it.

_____

....
....
....
....
....
....
....
....
....
....
....
....

_____

"That's one of the peculiar things about bad moods—we often fool ourselves and create misery by telling ourselves things that are simply not true."
                                                                —David Burns

Parenting

Many parents who have experienced personal hardship desire a better life for their children. To want to spare your children from having to go through unpleasant experiences is a noble aim, and it naturally stems from love and concern for the child. What these parents don't realize, however, is that while in the short term they may be making the lives of their children more pleasant, in the long term they may be preventing them from acquiring self-confidence, resilience, a sense of meaning, and important interpersonal skills. For healthy development, to grow and mature, the child needs to deal with some failure, struggle through some difficult periods, and experience some painful emotions.

Whether or not you are actually a parent, is your instinct to provide your children, or other children you care about, with as easy a life as possible? Think about the price a child who has everything pays for this "luxury."

....

....

....

....

....

....

....

....

WEEKLY GRATITUDE LIST

This week, I am grateful for:...

....

....

....

EXERCISE

The "Good Enough" Parent

Reflect on your relationship with a child—your own or someone else's. Make a list of opportunities where you had a chance to intervene in the child's life to make it easier. For each event, describe the outcome of your intervention or lack of intervention and reflect, in writing, on whether or not your decision was in the child's best interest. Think of opportunities to challenge the child, to allow him or her to struggle.

....

....

....

....

....

....

....

....

....

....

....

"Lucky parents who have fine children usually have lucky children who have fine parents."
—James A. Brewer

Check-In:
Looking Back

Reflecting on this journal so far, what have you implemented—or do you intend to implement—to make yourself happier? You can write about behavioral/habit change (such as expressing gratitude more frequently, simplifying your life, starting an exercise regimen, and so forth) or a change in your approach (such as giving yourself permission to be human, being more of a benefit finder, and so forth), or both.

What steps have you taken or will you take to make this change? What barriers might be stopping you from making the change, and how do you intend to overcome these barriers?

....
....
....
....
....
....
....
....
....
....
....

WEEKLY GRATITUDE LIST

This week, I am grateful for:...
....
....
....
....

"There isn't anything that isn't made easier through constant familiarity and training. Through training we can change; we can transform ourselves." —Dalai Lama

Post-Traumatic Growth

It is impossible to describe the pain that follows the loss of someone we loved. The person left behind to mourn is often unable to contemplate life without the deceased. However, what happens next varies drastically among individuals. Some people never recover from the loss. Others, after a period of grief, move on and are able to function as they did before, in terms of both their actions and their emotions. Finally, there are those who experience what Lawrence Calhoun and Richard Tedeschi call *post-traumatic growth*: the loss transforms them in profound ways—they appreciate life more, their relationships improve, and they become more resilient.

In his work on bereavement, Colin Murray Parkes describes how widows who do not express their emotions following the death of their husband suffer from longer-lasting and more severe physical and psychological symptoms than widows who "break down" after their loss. Jamie Pennebaker reports on studies that show that "the more people talked to others about the death of their spouse, the fewer health problems they reported having." After some time, while they continue to experience pain—and continue to accept it—they are able to go on with their lives. Giving ourselves the permission to feel, to break down if necessary, we are able to rise from the wreckage and create a larger emotional foundation, one better able to support us and those around us.

When Ralph Waldo Emerson was twenty-seven years old, his beloved wife, Ellen, died. Later, after he remarried and became a father, he lost his two-year-old son. Emerson wrote an essay titled "Compensation" that is a testament to his sense of life and optimism. Here is the last paragraph from the essay, which is essentially about posttraumatic growth:

> And yet the compensations of calamity are made apparent to the understanding also, after long intervals of time. A fever, a mutilation, a cruel disappointment, a loss of wealth, a loss of friends, seems at the moment unpaid loss, and unpayable. But the sure years reveal the deep remedial force that underlies all facts. The death of a dear friend, a wife, brother, lover, which seemed nothing but privation, somewhat later assumes the aspect of a guide or genius; for it commonly operates revolutions in our way of life, terminates an epoch of infancy or of youth which was waiting to be closed, breaks up a wonted occupation, or a household, or style of living, and allows the formation of new ones more friendly to the growth of character. It permits or constrains the formation of new acquaintances and the reception of new influences that prove of the first importance to the next years; and the man or woman who would have remained

a sunny garden-flower, with no room for its roots and too much sunshine for its head, by the falling of the walls and the neglect of the gardener is made the banian of the forest, yielding shade and fruit to wide neighborhoods of men.

How have you handled loss in the past, whether of a friend, a relationship, a job, or something else that was important to you?

....

....

....

....

....

....

....

....

WEEKLY GRATITUDE LIST

This week, I am grateful for: ....

....

....

....

EXERCISE

Mindfulness Meditation

Over the past few decades, an increasing amount of research has documented the benefits of mindfulness meditation for physical and mental health. Mindfulness is about being fully aware of whatever it is that we are doing and accepting (as much as possible) the present moment without judgment or evaluation. We are mindful when we focus on the here and now, experience the experience, allow ourselves to feel whatever feelings emerge regardless of whether or not we like what we are feeling.

Mindfulness meditation is the *practice* of acceptance. In the same way that understanding in theory what would improve your tennis backhand only helps you so far—you have to actually practice the moves in order to really become good at them—so theorizing about acceptance also has its limits.

While the practice of mindfulness meditation itself is simple, implementing it as a regular practice is anything but. For meditation to have a significant impact on the quality of your life, you need to meditate regularly, ideally every day, for at least ten minutes. However, a session every other day, or even once a week, is certainly better than nothing.

There are many variations on meditation, and attending a class led by an experienced instructor is a good idea. In the meantime, here are instructions for a simple meditation that you can start today.

Sit down, either on the floor or on a chair. Find a position that is comfortable for you, preferably with your back and neck straight. You may close your eyes if it helps you relax and concentrate.

Focus on your breathing. Inhale gently, slowly, and deeply. Feel the air going down all the way to your belly, and then exhale slowly and gently. Feel your belly rising as you breathe in, and then falling as you breathe out. For the next few minutes focus on your belly filling up with air as you inhale gently, slowly, and deeply, and then being emptied of air as you exhale slowly and gently. If your mind wanders to other places, kindly and calmly bring it back to the rise and the fall of your belly.

You are not trying to change anything. You are simply being.

"Mindfulness [involves] the complete 'owning' of each moment of your experience, good, bad, or ugly." —John Kabat-Zinn

Managing Expectations

n his book *Good to Great*, Jim Collins tells the story of Admiral James Stockdale, the highest-ranking American prisoner of war in Vietnam. Known for his unbreakable character and resilience, Stockdale described the two defining characteristics of American captives who were most likely to survive the brutal conditions of a Vietnamese prison. First, they openly faced and accepted, rather than ignored or dismissed, the harsh facts of their predicament. Second, they never stopped believing that they would some day get out. In other words, while they did not run away from the reality of the brutal truths about their current condition, they never lost hope that it would all work out in the end. By contrast, both those who believed that they would never get out and those who believed that they would be freed within an unrealistically short period of time were unlikely to survive.

Finding that balance between, on the one hand, high hopes and great expectations and, on the other, harsh reality, applies to goal setting in general. Although there is no simple technique that we can apply to identify which goals are realistic and capable of inspiring us, psychologist Richard Hackman suggests that "the right place to be for maximum motivation is wherever it is that you have a fifty-fifty chance of success."

Think of goals that you have set in the past. Were they realistic or unrealistic goals? Which goals inspired you and which elicited anxiety? Which goals energized you and which ones enervated you?

....

....

....

....

....

....

....

....

WEEKLY GRATITUDE LIST

This week, I am grateful for: ....

....

....

....

EXERCISE

Managing Goals

Think of up to five goals you already have, whether professional (a promotion, for instance) or personal (for example, increasing the number of times you work out each week). Make a list of these goals and note for each one whether it is attainable or challenging (or both).

	Attainable?	Challenging?
Goal 1	_____	_____
Goal 2	_____	_____
Goal 3	_____	_____
Goal 4	_____	_____
Goal 5	_____	_____

Now, if necessary, modify your list so that each goal is both attainable and challenging. Think of at least two new goals that will stretch you and yet be realistic.

"To travel hopefully is a better thing than to arrive."

—Robert Louis Stevenson

Self-Compassion

There is considerable research pointing to the importance of self-esteem when dealing with difficult experiences. Recently, however, psychologist Mark Leary and his colleagues have illustrated that especially in hard times, compassion toward the self is actually more beneficial than self-esteem. Leary explains: "Self-compassion helps people not to add a layer of self-recrimination on top of whatever bad things happen to them. If people learn only to feel better about themselves but continue to beat themselves up when they fail or make mistakes, they will be unable to cope non-defensively with their difficulties."

Self-compassion includes being understanding and kind toward yourself, mindfully accepting painful thoughts and feelings, and recognizing that your difficult experiences are part of being human. It is also about being forgiving toward yourself when you perform poorly on an exam, make a mistake at work, or get upset when you shouldn't have. Leary notes that "American society has spent a great deal of time and effort trying to promote people's self-esteem when a far more important ingredient of well-being may be self-compassion."

When the Dalai Lama and some of his followers began to work with Western scientists, they were surprised to find that self-esteem was an issue—that so many Westerners did not love themselves and that self-hate was pervasive. The discrepancy between self-love and love for others—between miserliness toward ourselves and generosity toward our neighbors—simply does not exist in Tibetan thought. In the words of the Dalai Lama, "Compassion, or *tsewa*, as it is understood in the Tibetan tradition, is a state of mind or way of being where you extend how you relate to yourself toward others as well." When the Dalai Lama was then asked to clarify whether indeed the object of compassion may be the self, he responded: "Yourself first, and then in a more advanced way the aspiration will embrace others. In a way, high levels of compassion are nothing but an advanced state of that self-interest. That's why it is hard for people who have a strong sense of self-hatred to have genuine compassion toward others. There is no anchor, no basis to start from."

Are you compassionate toward yourself? Where in your life can you be more compassionate, more forgiving?

....

....

....

....

....

....

....

....

WEEKLY GRATITUDE LIST

This week, I am grateful for:..

....

....

....

....

EXERCISE

●● Sentence Completion

On a separate piece of paper, complete the following sentence stems as quickly as possible; try not to think too much before you write. After you have completed them, look at your responses, reflect on them, and, in writing, consider what you can learn about yourself. You can repeat the same sentence stems each day this week or come up with your own stems.

- *If I love myself 5 percent more . . .*
- *To increase my self-esteem . . .*
- *To become 5 percent more compassionate toward myself . . .*
- *To become 5 percent more compassionate toward others . . .*
- *I am beginning to see that . . .*

....

....

....

....

....

....

....

....

....

....

....

....

....

....

....

....

....

....

"To say 'I love you' one must first be able to say the 'I.'" —Ayn Rand

Aging Gracefully

To lead happier, healthier, and longer lives we need to change our perception of aging by accepting reality for what it is. Whether we like it or not, we change over time—in some ways for the better, in others for the worse. Physically, we become slower and less agile as we age; over time, our libido weakens and we acquire more wrinkles. At the same time, aging provides us with tremendous intellectual, emotional, and spiritual opportunities for growth.

My intention is not to romanticize old age but simply to make it real, both the good and the bad. It is, of course, true that growing old, at times, can bring about difficulties, such as ill health, impacting the elderly person in unexpected and unwanted ways. But it is equally true that there are potential benefits that come with age. What we are able to see and understand, know and appreciate, when we're sixty or eighty is different from what we're capable of when we are twenty or thirty. There are no shortcuts to emotional and mental maturity; wisdom, judiciousness, intelligence, and perspective potentially develop with time and experience. Healthy aging is about actively accepting the real challenges that come with age, while appreciating the real opportunities that arise as we grow older.

In what ways have you developed and improved over time, with age? How do you hope to continue to do so?

....

....

....

....

....

....

....

....

WEEKLY GRATITUDE LIST

This week, I am grateful for: ....

....

....

....

....

EXERCISE

Learning from Elders

Engage in conversations with people who are older than you or have more experience than you have in one area or another. Ask them about their life experiences—their mistakes and their triumphs—and what they have learned from them. Listen—really listen—to what they have to say. Reflect, in writing, about what you have learned from them.

While I do not advocate that we put our critical faculties aside as we absorb the advice of other people, young or old, I do advocate being open to the wisdom that can only come with experience. Not only will we learn a great deal about our lives, but we are also more likely to appreciate the elderly and thus cultivate a more positive view of old age.

....

....

....

....

....

....

....

....

....

....

"How pleasant is the day when we give up striving to be young—or slender."
—William James

Being Real

n his book *Radical Honesty*, Brad Blanton writes: "We all lie like hell. It wears us out. It is the major source of all human stress. Lying kills people." For most people—the psychopath being an exception—lying is stressful, which is why lie detectors generally work. When we hide part of ourselves, when we lie about how we feel, the normal stress associated with lying is compounded by the stress of suppressing our emotions. Conversely, when we acknowledge how we feel—to ourselves and to those close to us—we are more likely to experience the calm that comes with honesty, the release and relief that comes with giving ourselves the permission to be human.

In a recent report published in Germany, people who have to smile for a living (such as store assistants and flight attendants) were found to be more prone to depression, stress, cardiovascular problems, and high blood pressure. Most people need to put on a mask for at least part of the day; basic human courtesy requires that we sometimes curb our emotions, whether anger or frustration or passion. The solution to this problem—whether you are required to pretend for much of the day (because you work in the service industry) or just some of the day (because you interact with other people, like everyone else in the world)—is to find what Brian Little calls a "restorative niche." The niche can be sharing your feelings with a trusted friend, writing whatever comes to mind in a personal journal, or simply spending time alone in your room. Depending on their constitution, some people may need ten minutes to recover from the emotional deception, while others may need a lot longer. The key during the recovery period is to be real, fully yourself, to do away with pretense and to allow yourself to feel any emotion that arises.

Where in your life are you required to put on an emotional mask? Where and with whom in your life can you create restorative niches?

This week, I am grateful for:...

....

....

....

....

EXERCISE

●● Sentence Completion

On a separate sheet of paper, generate at least six endings to each of the following sentence stems, as quickly as you can, without analyzing or thinking too much. After you have completed them, look at your responses, reflect on them, and, in writing, commit to action.

- *To be 5 percent more open about my feelings . . .*
- *If I am more open about my feelings . . .*
- *If I bring 5 percent more awareness to my fears . . .*
- *When I hide my emotions . . .*
- *To become 5 percent more real . . .*

....

....

....

....

....

....

....

_____

"Never apologize for showing feeling. When you do so, you apologize for the truth." —Benjamin Disraeli

The Unknown

e fear the unknown. We seek certainty in the present, to know what our life is really about right now. More than bad news, we fear no news; an uncertain diagnosis often feels worse to us than a certain, albeit negative one. More than mere curiosity, our desire to know is a deep existential need—for if knowledge is power, then its absence implies weakness.

The discovery—or, as some would argue, the invention—of God alleviates the anxiety that comes with not knowing. Mortals who promise certainty are crowned kings. When our future is threatened, as in times of war, we follow the leader who promises us the comfort of definitive knowledge. When we are sick, we put the doctor on a pedestal. As children, we look to seemingly omniscient adults to reduce our anxiety. Later, once our parents' imperfections are revealed, they are replaced by God, Guru, or Guide.

And yet deep down we experience anxiety, because deep down we know that we do not know. History, archaeology, and psychology cannot fully explain our collective and private pasts. Vivid descriptions of the afterlife, next month's horoscope, and, alas, even fortune cookies do not provide us with a clear picture of what tomorrow, or the day after, will bring. And when we really think about it we have no clue what the present is all about.

So what can we do? We need to accept—even celebrate—that we don't know. We must embrace uncertainty in order to feel more comfortable in its presence. Then, once we feel comfortable with our ignorance, we are better prepared to reconstruct our discomfort with the unknown into a sense of awe and wonder. It is about relearning to perceive the world—our lives—as a miracle unfolding.

What are you in awe of? Where and when do you experience the world as a miracle?

....

....

....

....

....

....

....

....

WEEKLY GRATITUDE LIST

This week, I am grateful for:...

....

....

....

....

EXERCISE

Just Walk

The late Phil Stone, one of the pioneers of positive psychology, was much more than my teacher. Beyond sharing his vast knowledge of the social sciences with me, he was extremely generous with his time when it came to counseling and supporting me. He is my role model for the kind of teacher I try to be to my students.

In 1999 Phil took me with him to Lincoln, Nebraska, to attend the first-ever Positive Psychology Summit. The second day of the conference was a clichéd September day—the sky was partly cloudy, the breeze warm, pleasant. After the morning lectures Phil said to me: "Let's go for a walk."

"Walk where?" I asked.

"Just walk."

It was one of the most important lessons I have ever learned.

Go for a walk outside, without a specific agenda other than to slow down—to experience and savor and appreciate the richness of our world. Simply take your time, as you sense the pulse of the city, the calm of a village, the expansiveness of the ocean, or the richness of the woods. Make *just walking* a regular ritual.

Helen Keller tells a story about her friend who had just returned from a long walk in the woods. When Keller asked her friend what she had observed, she replied, "Nothing in particular." Keller writes:

> I wondered how it was possible to walk for an hour through the woods and see nothing of note. I who cannot see find hundreds of things: the delicate symmetry of a leaf, the smooth skin of a silver birch, the rough, shaggy bark of a pine. I who am blind can give one hint to those who see: use your eyes as if tomorrow you will have been stricken blind. Hear the music of voices, the songs of a bird, the mighty

strains of an orchestra as if you would be stricken deaf tomorrow. Touch each object as if tomorrow your tactile sense would fail. Smell the perfume of flowers, taste with relish each morsel, as if tomorrow you could never taste or smell again. Make the most of every sense. Glory in all the facets and pleasures and beauty which the world reveals to you.

....

....

....

....

....

....

....

....

....

....

....

....

"The invariable mark of wisdom is to see the miraculous in the common." —Ralph Waldo Emerson

Learning from Jealousy

When the CEO of a company I had been consulting for expressed interest in a leadership seminar, I asked one of my friends, who is an expert on leadership and an excellent speaker, for help. My friend and I planned the seminar together, then shared the teaching between us. Watching my friend interact with my client, seeing how captivated the participants were by his eloquence, I began to regret having asked him to join me. I was jealous.

I was so upset with myself for feeling the way I did that I hardly slept for three nights. How could I feel jealousy toward a friend? How could I feel regret over asking him to work with me when I knew that everyone involved—myself and the participants—had learned so much from him? Finally, I decided to tell him what I felt—part confession, part request for advice. He told me that he too had felt jealous when he observed me teach. On that day, and for a long time after, we discussed our respective experiences of jealousy. Simply talking about it made us feel better and brought us closer together. Our only conclusion, though, was that jealousy is natural and, to some extent, unavoidable.

Neither my friend nor I chose to feel jealous—we had no say in the matter—but we did have a choice over our subsequent course of action. Our first choice was whether to *reject* or *accept* our emotional reaction, whether to suppress or acknowledge that which *is*. Our second choice was whether to *act* on our initial impulse (for instance, to stop collaborating with people we're jealous of) or whether to go beyond it (create as many alliances with competent people as we possibly can). The second choice is made significantly easier if we first choose to accept our feelings; negative emotions intensify and are more likely to control us if we try to suppress them.

If we refuse to accept that we can be jealous of a friend, we are more likely to behave badly toward him and then rationalize our behavior. Had I denied that my feelings toward my friend were driven by jealousy, I would have looked for an alternative explanation for my discomfort in his company. We are creatures of feeling and reason, and once we feel a certain way we have the need to find a reason for our feeling. Rather than dealing with the real reason for my emotional reaction, rather than admitting to feelings of which I did not approve, I would probably have justified my discomfort in his presence by finding fault with him. To avoid thinking ill of ourselves, we often condemn the people we have wronged.

Where in your life have you felt, or do you feel, jealousy or envy?
Observe the feeling, accept it without trying to change it—and
then commit to behaving in ways that you deem noble.

....

....

....

....

....

....

....

....

WEEKLY GRATITUDE LIST

This week, I am grateful for:...

....

....

....

....

EXERCISE

.•● Defensive Projection

There is much potential harm in suppressing unwanted thoughts or feelings. In their work on "Defensive Projection," psychologist Leonard Newman and his colleagues have shown that "when people are motivated to avoid seeing certain faults in themselves, they contrive instead to see those same faults in others." These unwanted thoughts and feelings become "chronically accessible," and we see them everywhere around us, in other people, even when they are not really there.

Make a list of five instances where you felt jealousy or envy, either in the past week or in the more distant past. Now, for each of the situations, try to either discuss that feeling with the person involved or write about it. The mere act of acknowledging jealousy or envy—through talking or writing about it—can help soften the emotion and help you rise above it.

....

....

....

....

....

....

....

....

....

"Acceptance of what has happened is the first step to overcoming the consequences of any misfortune."
—William James

Listening to Your Inner Voice

O ther people's voices and opinions can help us identify what we really, really want to do with our lives. These voices and opinions, however, can also get in the way of finding our true calling. It is not easy to identify the call of our calling, the voice of our vocation. And yet, to maximize our experience of happiness we need to identify our true intrinsic passions, the things we want to do independent of their impact on our social ratings. The experience of intrinsic motivation is central to the development of happiness as well as healthy self-esteem.

Where in your life are you true to yourself? Where do you feel that you still need to find your inner voice?

....

....

....

....

....

▓▓▓▓▓▓▓▓▓▓▓▓ **WEEKLY GRATITUDE LIST** ▓▓▓▓▓▓▓

This week, I am grateful for:..

....

....

....

....

EXERCISE

●◉ Spell of Anonymity

Imagine that a spell of anonymity is cast on you. For the rest of your life, and beyond, no one will know about the wonderful things that you are doing in this world. You will continue having daily interactions with your friends, but no matter what you do, they will all think that you are working at some mundane job that has no impact on other people's lives. You can do great deeds that contribute to others in a meaningful way, touch the hearts of millions around the world, volunteer in your community, help the elderly, yet no one will know that it was you who did these things. You can become the wealthiest person in the world but will not be able to flaunt any of your wealth. No one will thank you, no one will appreciate your work, no one will remind you how significant a life you are living, no one will know how rich you are. You, and you alone, will know how good you are.

In such a world, what would you do? What path, professional and personal, would you take?

After doing the exercise, reflect about the way your reaction is similar to or different from the way you actually live or intend to live your life. This exercise is not a prescription for how you should live your life, but only a way of raising awareness about some of the things that matter to *you* most.

....

....

....

....

....

....

....

....

....

....

....

....

"It is easy in the world to live after the world's opinion; it is easy in solitude to live after our own; but the great man is he who in the midst of the crowd keeps with perfect sweetness the independence of solitude."
                                                    —Ralph Waldo Emerson

The Law of Identity

From Aristotle's famous law of noncontradiction follows logically the law of identity, which states that something is itself: a person is a person, a cat is a cat, an emotion is an emotion, and so on. The law of identity is the foundation of logic and mathematics, and, by extension, of a coherent and meaningful philosophy. Without the law of noncontradiction or the law of identity, says Aristotle, it would be "absolutely impossible to have proof of anything: the process would continue indefinitely, and the result would be no proof of anything whatsoever." We could not even agree on the meaning of a word if we did not accept that something is itself. It is because we implicitly accept the law of identity that we can communicate and understand each other.

The law of identity is about recognizing that something is what it is, with all that this implies. In other words, there are facts inherent in existence that are what they are despite what a person—or six billion people—might wish them to be. Abraham Lincoln once asked, "How many legs does a dog have if you call the tail a leg?" His answer? "Four. Calling a tail a leg doesn't make it a leg." The law of identity may seem obvious, but it has relevance for the way we live our lives. All of us, not just philosophers, must *accept* the implications of this law: failure to recognize—and act upon the recognition—that something is itself can lead to dire consequences. If, for example, a person treats a *truck* as something that it's not—as, say, a *flower*—then this person is in danger of being run over. Similarly, if he deals with *cyanide* (poison) as if it were *food* (not poison), then he will most likely die.

While most people find it easy to respect the law of identity when it comes to physical objects like trucks or poison, many of us have a harder time when it comes to our feelings, especially if these feelings are unwanted because they threaten our sense of who we are. If it is important for me to see myself as brave, I may refuse to accept that I sometimes feel fear; if I think of myself as generous, it may be hard for me to accept feelings of envy. But if I am to enjoy psychological health, I need first of all to accept that I feel the way I do. *I need to respect reality.*

Think of experiences that you have had in which you or someone else failed to respect reality and ignored to some extent the law of identity. What was the outcome?

....

....

....

....

....

....

....

....

EXERCISE

.● ● Meditation

Allan Watts, the philosopher who has done much to bring Zen philosophy and practice to the West, writes, "The difference of the adept in Zen from the ordinary run of men is that the latter are, in one way or another, at odds with their humanity." In other words, Zen masters do not fight their nature but rather give themselves permission to be human. This Zen philosophy is very much in line with the idea of applying the law of identity to everyday life. Follow this guide to meditation on the permission to be human while keeping the tenets of the law of identity in mind:

Sit comfortably in a chair, or lie down if you prefer. If you're sitting down, plant your feet on the floor, comfortably relaxing. Close your eyes and shift your focus to your breathing. Take a deep breath in all the way down to your belly, then breathe out. Continue inhaling and exhaling, gently, calmly, slowly.

Now, shift your focus to your emotions, to your feelings. Regardless of your feeling at the moment—whether it's calm, happiness, anxiety, confusion, or boredom—shift your focus to the feeling and just observe it as you continue to breathe deeply into your belly.

Continue doing this for a few breaths. Whatever the emotion is, let it be there, flowing through you naturally.

Give yourself the permission, the space to be human. Now, in your mind's eye, imagine yourself leaving the place where you're sitting, going out to the street, or to your work, or any other place. See yourself walking and giving yourself the permission to be human, the freedom to experience whatever emotion comes up, whether it's fear or anxiety, whether it's joy and happiness. Life becomes so much lighter, so much simpler, when rather than trying to fight or defeat our nature, we accept our nature, we accept who we are. Return to your breathing while allowing whatever you are feeling to flow through you. On your next exhale, gradually, calmly open your eyes.

"Nature to be commanded must be obeyed."   —Francis Bacon

Self-Acceptance

Imagine a life of acceptance. Imagine spending a year in school—reading and writing and learning—without concern for the report card at the end of the year, accepting success and failure as natural components of learning and growing. Imagine being in a relationship without the need to mask imperfections. Imagine getting up in the morning and embracing the person in the mirror.

Acceptance, however, is not the panacea for perfectionism, and expecting it to work miracles will only lead to further unhappiness. In our search for a happier life through acceptance, we inevitably experience much turmoil. Swayed by promises of heaven on earth, lured by sirens in the odyssey toward self-acceptance, we look for perfect tranquility—and when we do not find it, we feel frustrated and disillusioned. And it is, indeed, an illusion that we can be perfectly accepting and hence perfectly serene. For can anyone living sustain the eternal tranquility of a Mona Lisa?

Why not be a little bit easier on ourselves and accept that to fail and to succeed are part of a full and fulfilling life, and that to experience fear, jealousy, and anger, and, at times, to be unaccepting of ourselves, is simply—and perfectly—human.

Can you think of a time when you felt totally accepting of yourself and your emotions? What was it that led to such a feeling? Can you feel full acceptance now?

....

....

....

....

....

....

....

....

■■■■■■■■■■■■■■■■ WEEKLY GRATITUDE LIST ■■■■■■■■■■■■■■■

This week, I am grateful for: ....

....

....

....

....

EXERCISE

Sentence Completion

On a separate sheet, generate at least six endings to each of the following sentence stems, as quickly as you can, without analyzing or thinking too much. After you have completed them, look at your responses, reflect on them, and, in writing, commit to action. Try to complete at least four sentence stems each day for the rest of this week.

- *If I give myself the permission to be human . . .*
- *When I reject my emotions . . .*
- *If I become 5 percent less of a Perfectionist . . .*
- *If I become 5 percent more realistic . . .*
- *If I become an Optimalist . . .*
- *If I appreciate my success 5 percent more . . .*
- *If I accept failure . . .*
- *I fear that . . .*
- *I hope that . . .*
- *I am beginning to see that . . .*

....

....

....

....

....

....

....

....

....

....

....

....

....

....

"The first step toward change is awareness. The second step is acceptance."

—Nathaniel Branden

Breaking Down Achievement

Professor Ellen Langer asked two groups of students to assess the intelligence of a number of highly accomplished scientists. The first group of students was given no information on how these scientists attained their success. Participants in this group rated the intelligence of the scientists as extremely high and did not perceive the scientists' achievements as attainable. Participants in the second group were exposed to the same scientists and the same achievements, but in addition they were told about the series of steps that the scientists took—the trials, errors, and setbacks on the road to scientific success. Students in this group evaluated these scientists as impressive—just like students in the first group did—but unlike participants in the first group, students in the second group evaluated the scientists' accomplishments as attainable.

When students in the first group were only exposed to the scientists' achievements, students entered the Perfectionist mind-set, looking at part of reality, the outcome; when students in the second group were exposed to the scientists' achievements as well as the series of steps that got them there, students entered the Optimalist mind-set, looking at reality as a whole, process and outcome.

Needless to say, all achievements come in a series of steps—people study for years, endure many failures, struggle, and experience ups and downs before they "make it." The music world, for example, is filled with "overnight successes" who naturally worked long and hard for many years before they got their big break. But when we look at the end result, we tend to discount the investments in energy and time that were required to get there, and the achievement appears to be beyond our reach—the work of a superhuman genius. As Langer writes, "By investigating how someone got somewhere, we are more likely to see the achievement as hard-won and our own chances as more plausible. . . . People can imagine themselves taking steps, while great heights seem entirely forbidding."

Think about a personal accomplishment. Reflect on what it took to get there—the ups and downs, the struggles and hardships.

....

....

....

....

....

....

....

....

WEEKLY GRATITUDE LIST

This week, I am grateful for: ....

....

....

....

....

EXERCISE

● ● Get Real!

Write down a goal that you care about, one that you are concerned you may not be able to achieve. Describe how you will reach this goal. Include in your story a description of the series of steps that you will take on the road to success, the obstacles and challenges that you will face, and how you will overcome them. Discuss where the pitfalls lie, where you may stumble and fall, and then how you will get up again. Finally, write about how you will eventually get to your destination. Make your story as vivid as possible, narrating it like an adventure story. Repeat this exercise for as many goals as you wish.

....

....

....

....

....

....

....

....

....
....
....
....
....
....
....
....

"Genius is 1 percent inspiration and 99 percent perspiration."
—Thomas Edison

Relationships:
Beautiful Enemies

I n his revolutionary work, *The Subjection of Women*, nineteenth-century English philosopher John Stuart Mill called for the liberation of women. He argued that "the principle which regulates the existing social relations between the two sexes—the legal subordination of one sex to the other—is wrong in itself, and now one of the chief hindrances to human improvement." Only when a man and a woman are equal can they "enjoy the luxury of looking up to the other, and can have alternately the pleasure of leading and of being led in the path of development." In healthy relationships, the man and the woman, at different times, take the lead and further the development of their partner.

The notion of leading and being led applies not only to the relationship between a man and a woman, but to any other intimate relationship as well. In his essay *Friendship*, Ralph Waldo Emerson recognized opposition as a necessary precondition for a friendship. In a friend, Emerson wrote, he was not looking for a "mush of concessions" or "trivial conveniency," in other words, for someone who would agree with everything he said. Rather, he was looking for a "*beautiful enemy*, untamable, devoutly revered."

A person who only wants to be "beautiful" and supportive of me without ever resisting or challenging what I do and say does not push me to improve and grow; a person who disputes what I say and do without caring and supporting me, is antagonistic and harsh. A true friend must be both beautiful toward me and be my enemy. A beautiful enemy challenges my behavior and my words, and at the same time unconditionally accepts my person. A beautiful enemy is someone who respects and loves me enough to question my ideas and behaviors; at the same time, her opposition to any of my words or actions does not change how much she cares for me as a person.

Who are the beautiful enemies in your life? In what ways have they helped you? How can you become more of a beautiful enemy to others?

EXERCISE

Conflict Resolution

Think of a conflict, major or minor, you have with someone. In writing, reframe the conflict by asking yourself how it contributes to or takes away from the ultimate currency, for you and for the other person. Elaborate on possible solutions that could maximize the overall level of happiness that you and the other person or group enjoy.

Would forgiveness or simply letting go be the best solution? Some conflicts exact a very high price from us, and holding on to them may just not be worth it in the ultimate currency. Not all conflicts can be resolved through this simple reframing—if only it were that easy—however, for one reason or another many people hold on to conflicts, with family members, ex-friends, or entire groups, that are unnecessary and exact a very high price from all those involved.

For example, is it worth my while to hold a grudge against someone who was a friend and let me down? Is it making me, and her, happier? Should I perhaps raise this topic and, after acknowledging that I was hurt, do what I can to resume the friendship which was, and could possibly still be, a source of the ultimate currency?

....

....

....

....

....

....

....

....

....

....

....

....

"He that wrestles with us strengthens our nerves, and sharpens our skill. Our antagonist is our helper." —Edmund Burke

Fixed Mind-Sets and Growth Mind-Sets

As defined by psychologist Carol Dweck, a fixed mind-set is the belief that our abilities—our intelligence, physical competence, personality, and interpersonal skills—are essentially set in stone and cannot really change. We are either gifted and talented, in which case we'll succeed in school, at work, in sport, and in our relationships, or we are permanently deficient and consequently doomed to failure. In contrast, a growth mind-set is the belief that our abilities are malleable—that they can, and do, change throughout our lives; we are born with certain abilities, but these provide a mere starting point, and to succeed we have to apply ourselves, dedicate time, invest a great deal of effort.

In a seminal study of fifth graders, Dweck showed that she was able to induce fixed or growth mind-sets with a single sentence. She repeatedly found that the students that were praised for their effort, rather than their intelligence, performed better on the same tasks and were also happier. Her findings are both disturbing (because they show how much impact ordinary words that we utter can have on our children) and encouraging (because we know how we can easily make a significant and positive impact). We need to praise children for their efforts—for that which is under their control—rather than for their intelligence, which is not.

Think about an ability or skill that you have improved over time as a result of your efforts. It could be anything from your ability on the tennis court to your speaking skills, from your courage to your empathy. What did you do to improve this ability?

WEEKLY GRATITUDE LIST

This week, I am grateful for:

EXERCISE

●● Changing to a Growth Mind-Set

We all have ideas about where our skills lie and about our own limitations. These ideas—that we are poor at math, that we are easily offended, that we aren't good at making decisions—can often take root very early in life and are hard to dismiss once they've become a part of what you perceive as your "self."

Think back to some early experiences where you became discouraged about your own abilities or skills based on something someone told you, or something that you told yourself. Write down five things that you at some point became resigned to not being skilled at—be it public speaking, athletics, or cooking. Now write the reason, if you can remember, why you reached this conclusion about yourself. Are these reasons rational? Are there things you would like to change, to do better, to work on, to improve?

....

....

....

....

....

....

....

....

....

....

"You are the embodiment of the information you choose to accept and act upon. To change your circumstances you need to change your thinking and subsequent actions."
                                                                —Adlin Sinclair

The Praised Generation

When I was in Australia last year, I happened to listen to a radio program in which a group of business leaders were complaining about the most recent crop of university graduates. These smart, well-educated twenty-somethings entering the workforce needed endless pampering and praise, and when criticized they would often sulk or even quit their jobs. Managers in the United States and throughout the Western world are facing the same problem. To the older generation, many of whom were educated in the school of hard knocks, the phenomenon of the spoiled and weak newcomer spells trouble.

Carol Dweck calls these newcomers "the praised generation." They are often the product of well-meaning parents and teachers who, out of a desire to raise the children's self-esteem, tended to offer constant and unconditional praise (to strengthen the ego) while refraining from any form of criticism (which might damage the fragile ego). The results, however, were often the opposite of those intended: instead of becoming adults with high self-esteem, the children turned out to be insecure and spoiled. According to Dweck, "We now have a workforce full of people who need constant reassurance and can't take criticism. Not a recipe for success in business, where taking on challenges, showing persistence, and admitting and correcting mistakes are essential."

How do you praise children and adults? Do you focus on effort and process? Can you think of examples of teachers you had, or your children have, who exemplify the path to a more secure adulthood?

....

....

....

....

....

....

....

....

....

....

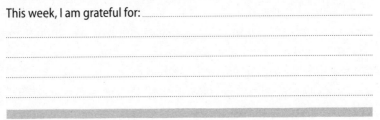

WEEKLY GRATITUDE LIST

This week, I am grateful for: ....

....

....

....

....

EXERCISE

●● My Best Teacher

Write about the best teacher you've ever had. It could be your parent, a first-grade teacher, a college professor, or a boss who invested a great deal in your professional development. What was it about this teacher that brought out the best in you? What can you learn from that teacher when it comes to dealing with your own or others' children?

Now think about how you function as a teacher in various areas in your life. How can you apply the lessons you learned from your teacher in the workplace, at home, in other areas of your life? You can repeat the exercise, this time reflecting on another teacher and comparing him or her to the first one. What are some of the similarities and differences between the two? What else can you learn about effective teaching that you can apply to your role as a teacher?

"It is doubtful whether any heavier curse could be imposed on man than the complete gratification of all his wishes without effort on his part, leaving nothing for his hopes, desires, or struggles."
—Samuel Smiles

Making Decisions

Early on in his career, Jim Burke, the highly successful CEO of Johnson & Johnson for thirteen years until his retirement in 1989, learned the importance of learning from mistakes from General Johnson. After Burke developed a new product that turned out to be a total dud, he was called in by General Johnson, who was chairman of the board at the time. Burke expected to be fired. Instead, General Johnson extended his hand and said:

> I just want to congratulate you. All business is making decisions, and if you don't make decisions you won't have any failures. The hardest job I have is getting people to make decisions. If you make the same decision wrong again, I'll fire you. But I hope you'll make a lot of others, and that you'll understand there are going to be more failures than successes.

Burke went on to embrace the same philosophy when he became CEO: "We don't grow unless we take risks. Any success-

ful company is riddled with failures." Before joining Johnson &
Johnson, Burke had failed at three other businesses. By making
his failures public, by telling and retelling the story of his encoun-
ter with General Johnson, Burke sent an important message to his
employees.

*Think about an error that was made at an organization you
worked for or that you know well. What was learned from the
mistake? What more could have been learned? Do you know a
leader who creates an environment that is conducive to learning
from mistakes? What are some of the specific things that this
leader does?*

....
....
....
....
....
....
....
....

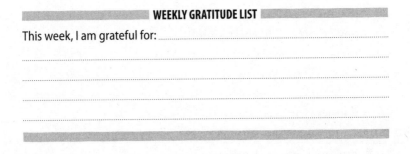

WEEKLY GRATITUDE LIST

This week, I am grateful for:..
....
....
....

EXERCISE

● ● Learning from Mistakes

It's natural to resist making decisions that could lead to failure—we all do it. Yet time and time again history shows that those who succeed are usually the ones who failed time and again before making their big breakthrough.

Think of your current occupation, be it raising a family or running a company. Write down the three biggest mistakes you've made in the past year, mistakes that are a direct result of decisions you've made. Now, next to each, list the corresponding lessons or insights you've gained from making these mistakes. Put the list somewhere you can see it and reread it periodically as a reminder that these mistakes can often be our most opportune moments to learn.

....

....

....

....

....

....

....

....

....

....

....

....

....

"If you want to increase your success rate, double your failure rate."

—Thomas J. Watson

Psychological Safety

Amy Edmondson, now a professor at Harvard Business School, worked as a doctoral student with Professor Richard Hackman, one of the leading scholars in the field of organizational behavior. In her research, Edmondson wanted to show that hospital staff who were members of teams that met Hackman's conditions for effective teamwork—conditions such as clear and compelling goals and appropriate resources—were less likely to make medical errors.

However, Edmondson's research yielded surprising results. Teams that met Hackman's conditions for effectiveness seemed to make *more* mistakes, rather than fewer. This contradicted decades of research. What was going on? How could this be? And then it dawned on her that the good teams "don't make more mistakes, they report more."

Amy went back to the hospital to test her revised hypothesis, and what she found was indeed that the teams that met Hackman's conditions for success were making significantly fewer errors. Because members of the teams that did not meet these conditions were concealing their errors, to the outside observer it seemed that they were making fewer errors, when in fact they were making more. It was only with respect to errors that could not be concealed—such as the death of a patient—that it was clear which teams were getting it wrong more often.

Edmondson's research took the concept of "learn to fail or fail to learn" from the individual realm and applied it to groups and organizations. In a world where change is the only constant, where personal improvement and organizational learning are essential for competitiveness, fear of reporting a failure is a recipe for long-term failure. Well-led teams, Edmondson discovered, enjoyed *psychological safety*, the confidence that no member of the team would be embarrassed or punished if she spoke out, asked for assistance, or failed in a specific task. When team leaders create a climate of psychological safety, when members feel comfortable "failing" and then sharing and discussing their mistakes, all members of the team can learn and improve. In contrast, when mistakes are concealed, learning is less likely to take place, and the likelihood that errors will be repeated is higher.

Think of a place where you experienced psychological safety. It could be in your workplace, past or present, at home with your parents, or in class with a particular teacher. What were you like, and how were you different compared to other places where you did not experience psychological safety?

....

....

....

....

....

....

....

....

WEEKLY GRATITUDE LIST

This week, I am grateful for:...

....

....

....

EXERCISE

●● Creating a Safe Place

Do you create a psychologically safe environment for the people around you, be they your children, employees, friends, or partner? While we usually attribute people's behaviors to their personal characteristics, their actions are often a result of the environment in which they function. The same child, for example, will behave very differently depending on the environment.

What brought out the best in you, as a child and as an adult? Now write about the conditions you need to put in place in order to create a healthy environment, one that will bring out the best in people around you.

....

....

....

....

....

....

....

....

....

....

....

....

"Freedom is not worth having if it does not connote freedom to err."
—Mahatma Gandhi

Relationships: In the Bedroom

avid Schnarch, whose work has revolutionized the area of marriage counseling and sex therapy, points out that sex can actually get better with time. As Schnarch puts it, "cellulite and sexual potential are highly correlated." Our potential to peak sexually is greater when we are in our fifties or sixties, and sex with the partner we've been with for decades can be significantly better than with a new person. This flies in the face of conventional wisdom. After all, sexual arousal is generally higher at twenty-four than at sixty-four, and our physical reaction is more pronounced when encountering a sexy stranger than it is when we see our partner of three decades. However, as Schnarch points out, great sex is not the product of the immediate biological, physiological response to our partner; great sex combines our hearts and minds in addition to our bodies.

Schnarch contrasts *"genital prime*—the peak years of physical reproductive maturity—with *sexual prime*—the specifically human capacity for adult eroticism and emotional connection." And when it comes to sexual prime, older can be better: "If you want intimacy during sex, there isn't a sixteen-year-old that can keep up with a healthy sixty-year-old. People are capable of much better sex and intimacy as they mature."

Because after a certain age there is gradual physical decline—the fifty-year-old body cannot do everything that a body half its age is capable of—the person who does not recognize the difference between sex as a purely physical act and sex as encompassing both mind and body may assume a *decline mind-set*. While the growth mind-set suggests that sex gets better with time and the fixed mind-set that sex does not change, the person with the decline mind-set expects sex to get worse over time. The decline mind-set takes away from the joy of sex and becomes a self-fulfilling prophecy: sex really does get worse.

What do you need to do to bring more joy to the bedroom? What do you need to let go of?

░░░░░░░░░░░░░░░ **WEEKLY GRATITUDE LIST** ░░░░░░░░░░░░░░░

This week, I am grateful for: ....

....

....

....

....

EXERCISE

Learning from Thriving Relationships

Interview two people who are in a thriving long-term relationship. (They can be partners or in two separate relationships.) Keep in mind that there are no perfect relationships, and that you are looking for relationships from which you can learn. Each interview can last for anywhere between fifteen minutes and a full hour. Some questions you may want to consider asking are: What makes for successful relationships? How has your relationship helped you grow as a person? How do you deal with conflict? What works in your relationship? What advice would you give about cultivating a healthy relationship?

Write about what you've learned from these interviews, and then add your own thoughts and feelings about what it takes to create a thriving long-term relationship.

....

....

....

....

....

....

....

....

....

....

....

....

"There are few stronger predictions of happiness than a close, nurturing, equitable, intimate, lifelong companionship with one's best friend."
—David Myers

Settling for "Good Enough"

When I was in my twenties, the passionate Perfectionist in me wanted it all, and to some extent I felt that I could indeed have it all. I spent long hours at work, had some social life, and was overall content with my work-life *im*balance. Then I married and had children and the earth suddenly seemed to accelerate; as my priorities changed there was suddenly not enough time to do what I wanted to do. I felt increasingly frustrated both at home and at work. There was so much more I wanted to accomplish and experience, and yet no matter how hard I worked, no matter how much time I spent with my family, I felt I was not doing enough.

Reflecting on my overall situation, I identified five areas in my life where it was important for me to thrive: as a parent, as a partner, professionally, as a friend, and in the area of personal health. These five areas did not encompass all the things that I cared about in life, but they were the most significant ones to me, the ones that I wanted to spend most of my time on.

I adopted a new approach to my life, and instead of trying to do it all, I asked myself what would be *good enough* in each of the five areas of my life that were important to me. In a perfect world I would be spending twelve hours a day engaged in my work; in the real world, nine to five was good enough, even if it meant turning down some opportunities I would have liked to pursue. In a perfect world I would be practicing yoga for ninety minutes six times a week and spending a similar amount of time at the gym; in the real world, an hour of yoga twice a week and jogging for thirty minutes three times a week was good enough. Similarly, going out with my wife once a week, meeting friends once a week, and spending the remaining evenings at home with my wife and kids was far short of my Perfectionist ideal, but it would (have to) do. All this was, as far as I could see, the optimal solution—the best I could do given the various demands and the constraints of my life.

It was a great relief to adopt this new *good-enough* approach. With my revised set of expectations, a fresh sense of satisfaction replaced the old frustration. And, unexpectedly, I found that I was more energized and focused.

*What are the areas of your life that are most important to you? Do you think you could fit these areas into a **good-enough** model?*

....

....

....

....

▓▓▓▓▓▓▓▓▓▓▓▓▓▓▓▓ **WEEKLY GRATITUDE LIST** ▓▓▓▓▓▓▓▓▓▓▓▓▓▓▓▓

This week, I am grateful for:..

....

....

....

....

▓▓

EXERCISE

●● Good Enough

Make a list of the most important areas in your life. You can use categories such as *Professional, Family, Romantic, Friends, Health, Travel, Hobby, Art,* or others. First note under each category what you would *ideally* like to do and how much time you would *ideally* like to spend. Then, for each category distinguish between the part that you can give up and the part that you see as indispensable. Write down the indispensable activities under your *good-enough* list. For example, under *Work,* your ideal might be eighty hours a week. Given other constraints and desires, that may not be realistic. Good enough for you might be fifty hours a week. Ideal in the *Friends* category might be meeting friends every night after work; good enough might be two evenings a week. In a perfect world, you would play fifteen rounds of golf a month; three rounds a month, though, might be good enough.

Category	Ideal	Good Enough
Work	*Eighty-hour weeks*	*Fifty-hour weeks*
Friends	*Daily get-togethers*	*Two weekly get-togethers*
Golf	*A round every other day*	*Three rounds a month*

After you introduce these changes, revisit your list once in a while. Are you trying to do too much? Too little? What has changed? Is the compromise that you have made in one area of your life making you unhappy? Could you do a little more there and perhaps a little less in another area? There are no easy formulas for finding the optimal balance. Moreover, our needs and wants change over time, as we change and as our situation changes. Be attentive to your inner needs and wants, as well as to the external constraints.

....

....

....

....

....

....

....

....

....

....

....

....

"How we spend our days is how we spend our lives."

—Annie Dillard

Money and Happiness

Nobel Prize winner in economics Daniel Kahneman has, over the past few years, turned his attention to studying happiness. In their research, Kahneman and his colleagues found little support for the connection between wealth and happiness. According to one of their studies, the results of which were published in *Science* magazine,

> The belief that high income is associated with good mood is widespread but mostly illusory. People with above-average income are relatively satisfied with their lives but are barely happier than others in moment-to-moment experience, tend to be more tense, and do not spend more time in particularly enjoyable activities. Moreover, the effect of income on life satisfaction seems to be transient. We argue that people exaggerate the contribution of income to happiness because they focus, in part, on conventional achievements when evaluating their life or the lives of others.

Surprisingly, some people feel more depressed once they have attained material prosperity than they did while striving for it. The rat racer is sustained by the hope that his actions will yield some future benefit, which makes his negative emotions more bearable. However, once he reaches his destination and realizes that material prosperity does not make him happy, there is nothing to sustain him. He is filled with a sense of despair and hopelessness because there is nothing else to look forward to, nothing that would allow him to envision a future in which he would be happy.

In making decisions and judgments, we also tend to focus on the material rather than paying heed to the emotional because those things that are quantifiable lend themselves more easily to assessment and evaluation. We value the measurable—material wealth and prestige—over the immeasurable: emotions and meaning.

Does concern over wealth and prestige take away from your overall experience of happiness? In what ways? How can this change?

WEEKLY GRATITUDE LIST

This week, I am grateful for: ....

....

....

....

....

EXERCISE

●● Happiness List

Take some time to think about activities that make you happy. Then create a list of the top five things you can do every week that provide you (or could provide you) with the most happiness and fulfillment. Are you spending sufficient time engaged in these activities? If at all possible, commit to doing more of them by putting time aside in your datebook or by making the necessary arrangements to make this investment in the ultimate currency happen.

Once you have the list, estimate how much each activity costs each week in terms of dollars. Have you noticed that many of the activities you value are the ones that don't cost you anything other than time? Put the list somewhere you can see it, such as on your refrigerator or bathroom mirror, to remind yourself of what truly matters to you. The list can also be a reminder to you that the ultimate currency is within reach, and that while money can provide a sense of comfort, true happiness cannot be purchased with all the money in the world. Periodically, once a year or so, repeat this exercise.

....
....
....
....
....
....
....
....
....
....
....
....

"The chief value of money lies in the fact that one lives in a world in which it is overestimated."　　—H. L. Mencken

Self-Concordant Goals

oals pursued out of deep personal conviction and/or a strong interest are referred to as self-concordant. These goals, according to psychologists Kennon Sheldon and Andrew Elliot, are "integrated with the self" emanating "directly from self-choice." Generally, for goals to be self-concordant, the person has to feel that she chose them rather than that they were imposed on her, that they stem from a desire to *express* part of her self rather than from the need to *impress* others.

Research in this area indicates that there is a qualitative difference between the meaning we derive from extrinsic goods such as social status and the state of our bank account, and the meaning we derive from intrinsic goods such as personal growth and a sense of connection to others. Financial goals usually—though not always—are not self-concordant, stemming from an extrinsic rather than an intrinsic source.

While there are clearly many benefits to identifying and pursuing self-concordant goals, it is anything but easy. We need to first know what we want to do with our lives, and then to have the courage to be true to our wants.

What are some of your self-concordant goals? Are there any internal or external barriers that prevent you from pursuing these goals?

....

....

....

....

....

....

....

....

WEEKLY GRATITUDE LIST

This week, I am grateful for: ....

....

....

....

EXERCISE

Setting Self-Concordant Goals

People who articulate and pursue self-concordant goals are generally more successful as well as happier. Ask yourself what it is that you really, really want to do in each of the key areas of your life—from relationships to work. For each area, include the following:

- *Long-term goals. These are concrete objectives, with clear lifelines, for anywhere from one to thirty years down the line. These should be challenging goals; they should stretch you. Remember that it is less important for long-term happiness whether or not you actually achieve your goals; the primary objective of goals is to liberate you to enjoy the here and now, the journey.*
- *Short-term goals. This is about achieving the long-term goals by dividing them into manageable steps. What do you need to do, in the coming year, month, or day, in the service of the above goals?*
- *Action plan. In your calendar, put down the specific activities that you need to carry out, either as a regular weekly or daily undertaking (these are your rituals) or as a onetime activity.*

When we do not set explicit goals for ourselves, we are at the mercy of external forces—ones that come from the outside and rarely lead to self-concordant activities. The choice we face is between passively reacting to extrinsic demands and actively creating our life.

....

....

....

....

"Happiness grows less from the passive experience of desirable circumstances than from involvement in valued activities and progress toward one's goals."   —David Myers and Ed Diener

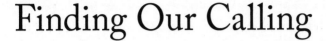

Finding Our Calling

The psychologist Abraham Maslow once wrote that "the most beautiful fate, the most wonderful good fortune that can happen to any human being, is to be paid for doing that which he passionately loves to do." It is not always easy to discover what sort of work might yield this "good fortune" in the ultimate currency. Research examining people's relation to their work can help.

Psychologist Amy Wrzesniewski and her colleagues suggest that people experience their work in one of three ways: as a job, as a career, or as a calling. A job is mostly perceived as a chore, with the focus being financial rewards rather than personal fulfillment. The person goes to work in the morning primarily because he feels that he has to rather than wants to. He has no real expectations from the job beyond the paycheck at the end of the week or month, and he mostly looks forward to Friday or a vacation.

The person on a career path is primarily motivated by extrinsic factors such as money and advancement—by power and prestige. She looks forward to the next promotion, to the next advancement up the hierarchy—from associate professor to tenured professor, from teacher to headmistress, from vice president to president, from assistant editor to editor in chief.

For a person experiencing his work as a calling, work is an end in itself. While the paycheck is certainly important, and advancement is too, he primarily works because he wants to. He is motivated by intrinsic reasons and experiences a sense of personal fulfillment; his goals are self-concordant. He is passionate about what he does and derives personal fulfillment from his work; he perceives it as a privilege rather than as a chore.

Do you see your work as a job, a career, or a calling? Ask the same question about other positions you held in the past.

....

....

....

....

....

....

....

....

WEEKLY GRATITUDE LIST

This week, I am grateful for: ....

....

....

....

EXERCISE

●●● The Three-Question Process

Write down your answers to the following questions, then find the overlap among the responses:

1. What is meaningful to me? In other words, what provides me a sense of purpose?

2. What is pleasurable to me? In other words, what do I enjoy doing?

3. What are my strengths? In other words, what am I good at?

Answering these questions can help you identify your path on the macro level (what your life calling is) as well as the micro level (what you would like your day-to-day to look like). While the two are interconnected, it is more difficult, and therefore takes more courage, to introduce the macrolevel change—such as leaving one's work or the safety of a known path. Microlevel changes, such as putting aside two weekly hours to practice one's hobby, are easier to introduce—and yet may also yield high dividends in the ultimate currency.

....

....

....

....

....

....

....

....

"Taste the joy that springs from labor."

—Henry Wadsworth Longfellow

Happiness Boosters

Most people go through spells of happiness drought. I have not met many students who enjoy exam period; even in the most engaging workplaces, some projects are less interesting than others. Whether it is out of necessity or by choice, for most of us there are periods when much of what we do does not afford us satisfaction. Fortunately, this does not mean that we need to resign ourselves to unhappiness during these times.

Meaningful and pleasurable activities can function like a candle in a dark room—and just as it takes a small flame or two to light up an entire physical space, one or two happy experiences during an otherwise uninspiring period can transform our general state. I call these brief but transforming experiences *happiness boosters*—activities that can last from a few minutes to a few hours and that provide us with both meaning and pleasure, both future and present benefit.

What are your happiness boosters?

....
....
....
....
....
....
....
....
....

▬▬▬▬▬▬▬ WEEKLY GRATITUDE LIST ▬▬▬▬▬▬▬

This week, I am grateful for:...
....
....
....
....

EXERCISE

Boosting Our Happiness

Generate a list of happiness boosters that you can then pursue throughout your week. These could include "general" boosters that you can do as a matter of routine (spending time with your family and friends, pleasure reading, and so on), as well as "exploratory" boosters that can help you find out whether to introduce a more significant change to your life (volunteering at a school once a week, for instance). Enter the boosters into your daily planner and, if possible, create rituals around them.

....

....

....

....

....

....

....

....

....

....

....

"Fill your life with as many moments and experiences of joy and passion as you humanly can. Start with one experience and build on it."
—Marcia Wexler

Depth of Happiness

The depth of our happiness is like the roots of a tree—providing the foundation, the constant element of our well-being. The height of our happiness is like the leaves—beautiful, coveted, and yet ephemeral, changing, and withering with the seasons. The question that many philosophers and psychologists have asked is whether the depth of our happiness can be changed or whether we are predestined to experience highs and lows around a fixed level.

While there is some genetic component to our happiness—some people are born with a happy disposition while others are not—our genes define a range, not a set point. Grumpy may not be able to cultivate the same view of life that Happy enjoys, and a natural-born whiner may not be able to transform himself into a Pollyanna, but we all can become significantly happier. And most people fall far short of their happiness potential.

In a review of the literature on happiness, Sonja Lyubomirsky, Kennon Sheldon, and David Schkade illustrate how a person's level of happiness is primarily determined by three factors: "a genetically determined set point for happiness, happiness-relevant circumstantial factors, and happiness-relevant activities and practices." While we have no control over our genetic predisposition, and sometimes little influence over the circumstances we find ourselves in, we usually have considerably more control over the kind of activities and practices that we pursue. This third category, according to Lyubomirsky and her colleagues, "offers the best opportunities for sustainably increasing happiness." Pursuing meaningful and pleasurable activities can significantly raise our levels of well-being.

Our pursuit of the ultimate currency can be a never-ending process of flourishing and growth; there is no limit to how much happiness we can attain. By pursuing work, education, and relationships that yield both meaning and pleasure, we become progressively happier—experiencing not just an ephemeral high that withers with the leaves, but lasting happiness with deep and stable roots.

What experiences or people in your life have contributed to your long-term happiness?

....

....

....

....

....

....

....

....

....

▬▬▬▬▬▬▬ **WEEKLY GRATITUDE LIST** ▬▬▬▬▬▬▬
This week, I am grateful for: ....

....

....

....

....

EXERCISE

●●● Appreciative Inquiry

In the 1980s David Cooperrider and his colleagues introduced a simple yet revolutionary approach to change that has since helped numerous individuals and organizations learn and grow. Rather than focusing on what doesn't work—as most intervention programs and consultants do—Appreciative Inquiry focuses on what does work, and then accentuates it. To appreciate literally means to recognize the value of something, and also to increase its value. Appreciating the positive makes us feel good and also helps to spread the good. We draw on the past to inspire the present and create a better future.

Do this exercise with a partner or in a small group (or, if you prefer, in writing). Take turns telling one another what has made you happier in the past—ten years ago, last month, or earlier in the day. It could be a meal, an evening with your family, a work project, or a concert. What specifically was it that made you feel good? Was it the connection you felt to other people? Was it the fact that you were challenged? Was it a sense of awe that you experienced?

Now think of a person you know well and whom you consider happy. Why do you think he or she is happy? What can you learn from him or her?

Finally, how can what you have learned—from your personal experience and the experience of others—inform your future actions? Make an actual commitment, a resolution, in writing and/or to the person doing the exercise with you.

....

....

....

....

....

....

....

....

....

....

....

....

"Happiness depends upon ourselves."   —Aristotle

Letting Our Light Shine

Our capacity for the pursuit of happiness is a gift of nature. No person, no religion, no ideology, no government has the right to take it away from us. We set up our political structures—our constitutions, our courts of law, our armies—to protect our right to pursue happiness freely. Yet nothing external can protect us from what I have come to believe is the greatest impediment we face in our pursuit of the ultimate currency—our feeling that we are somehow unworthy of happiness.

Why would anyone actively deprive himself of happiness? In her book *Return to Love*, Marianne Williamson provides insight into this quandary: "Our deepest fear is not that we are inadequate. Our deepest fear is that we are powerful beyond measure. It is our light, not our darkness, that most frightens us. We ask ourselves who am I to be brilliant, gorgeous, talented and fabulous? Actually, who are you not to be?"

To lead a happy life we must also experience a sense of worthiness. As Nathaniel Branden writes, "In order to seek values, man must consider himself worthy of enjoying them. In order to fight for his happiness, he must consider himself worthy of happiness." We must appreciate our core self, who we really are, independent of our tangible accomplishments; we must believe that we deserve to be happy; we must feel that we are worthy by *virtue* of our existence—because we are born with the heart and mind to experience pleasure and meaning.

When we do not accept our worth, we ignore or even actively undermine our talents, our potential, our joy, our accomplishments. Refusing to accept the good things that happen to us leads to unhappiness and, given that we are still unhappy despite all the potential sources of happiness in our lives, to nihilism.

Before we are able to receive a gift, from a friend or from nature, we have to be open to it; a bottle with its cap screwed on tightly cannot be filled with water no matter how much water we try to pour into it or how often we try—the water simply runs down its sides, never filling it. It is only when we feel worthy of happiness that we open ourselves up to life's ultimate treasure.

What, if any, internal and external factors are stopping you from finding happiness?

WEEKLY GRATITUDE LIST

This week, I am grateful for:

EXERCISE

Sentence Completion

Here are some sentence stems that can help you overcome some of the possible barriers to happiness. Complete them, as quickly as possible, without thinking or analyzing. At the end of each day, or at the end of the week, look over your responses and commit to action.

- *The things that stand in the way of my happiness . . .*
- *To feel 5 percent more worthy of happiness . . .*
- *If I refuse to live by other people's values . . .*
- *If I succeed . . .*
- *If I give myself the permission to be happy . . .*
- *When I appreciate myself . . .*
- *To bring 5 percent more happiness to my life . . .*
- *I am beginning to see that . . .*

Continue to do these and other sentence stems—from this book or from Nathaniel Branden's work—on a regular basis. The insights and behavioral changes that this simple exercise can generate are remarkable.

"Most people are about as happy as they make up their minds to be."

—Abraham Lincoln

The Wisdom of Perspective

You are one hundred and ten years old. A time machine has just been invented, and you are selected as one of the first people to use it. The inventor, a scientist from NASA, tells you that you will be transported back to the day when, as it happens, you first read *Even Happier*. You, with the wisdom of having lived and experienced life, have fifteen minutes to spend with your young and inexperienced self. What do you say when you meet? What advice do you give yourself?

I formulated this thought experiment after reading an account by psychiatrist Irvin Yalom of terminally ill cancer patients:

> An open confrontation with death allows many patients to move into a mode of existence that is richer than the one they experienced prior to their illness. Many patients report dramatic shifts in life perspective. They are able to trivialize the trivial, to assume a sense of control, to

stop doing things they do not wish to do, to communicate more openly with families and close friends, and to live entirely in the present rather than in the future or the past. As one's focus turns from the trivial diversions of life, a fuller appreciation of the elemental factors in existence may emerge: the changing seasons, the falling leaves, the last spring, and especially, the loving of others. Over and over we hear our patients say, "Why did we have to wait until now, till we are riddled with cancer, to learn how to value and appreciate life?"

What struck me about Yalom's and others' accounts of people finding themselves—beginning to live life fully, for the first time—is that following the news of their terminal disease, they were still the same people with the same knowledge of life's questions and answers, the same cognitive and emotional capacities. No one descended from Mount Sinai presenting them with commandments on how to live; no Greek sage or oracle revealed to them the secrets to the good life; no one injected them with mind- or heart-enhancing drugs; they did not discover a new and revolutionary self-help book that changed their lives.

Yet, with the same capacities they have always had—which seemed to be inadequate in making them happy before—their lives changed. They gained no new knowledge, but, rather, an acute awareness of what they knew all along. In other words, they had within them the knowledge of how they should live life. It was just that they ignored this knowledge or were not conscious of it.

*Have you had experiences that made you reevaluate your
priorities? Did you follow up on your new insights or
understanding?*

....

....

....

....

....

....

....

....

WEEKLY GRATITUDE LIST

This week, I am grateful for:...

....

....

....

....

EXERCISE

●●● Advice from Your Inner Sage

Do the exercise described above. Imagine that you are one hundred and ten years old—or significantly older than you are now. Take fifteen minutes to give yourself advice on how to find more happiness in your life, starting at this point. Do the exercise in writing. As much as possible, ritualize the advice. If, for instance, your older self advises you to spend more time with your family, commit to a weekly or biweekly family outing.

Regularly refer back to this exercise—look at what you wrote, add to it, ask yourself whether you have taken the advice of your inner sage.

....

....

....

....

....

....

....

....

....

....

....

....

....

"Life would be infinitely happier if we could only be born at the age of eighty and gradually approach eighteen."   —Mark Twain

Check-In: Looking Back

Now, reflecting on this journal in its entirety, what have you implemented, or do you intend to implement, to make yourself happier? Again, you can write about behavioral/ habit change (such as being on time for meetings, opening up to your partner, pursuing self-concordant goals, and so on) or a change in your approach (such as appreciating old age, being more compassionate toward yourself, and so on), or both.

What steps have you taken or will you take to make the change?
What barriers might be stopping you from making the change, and how do you intend to overcome these barriers?

....
....
....
....

WEEKLY GRATITUDE LIST

This week, I am grateful for: ....

....
....
....
....

"*The great end of life is not knowledge but action.*"

—Thomas Huxley

Daily Reminders

Go over your journal, from the beginning, and write down a few key points that you'd like to be reminded of now that the year is over. Each point should be followed by an explanatory sentence. The ideas can be taken directly from the journal or not. Here is a sample from my personal list:

- *Focus on the positive.* I am a benefit finder who seeks and creates good in the world.

- *Permission to be human.* I accept my emotions, the painful and the joyful, just as I accept the law of gravity.

- *Know and be known.* I create intimacy with my partner, family, and friends by sharing and expressing my authentic self.

- *Life is an adventure.* I experience the excitement and joy of the day-to-day.

- *Empathy and compassion.* I act with generosity and kindness toward myself and others.

- *Learn to fail or fail to learn.* I accept failures and mistakes as natural, and as opportunities for learning and growing.

Your list should have at least five bullet points and no more than twelve. These can be used after the journal is over to remind you of things to keep in mind. Ideally, you should create a ritual of reading them each morning or at least once a week.

_____

_____

_____

_____

_____

_____

_____

_____

_____

_____

_____

_____

_____

_____

_____

_____

_____

_____

_____

"I read and walked for miles at night along the beach, writing bad blank verse and searching endlessly for someone wonderful who would step out of the darkness and change my life. It never crossed my mind that that person could be me." —Anna Quindlen